THE MO~~T~~

DRUG PREVENTION

Lessons in Drug Prevention:
Handbook Two
All The Little Things We Say and Do

By
Miles To Go
Kelly Townsend, M.S. & Jonathan Scott

The Mother's Checklist of Drug Prevention
Lessons in Drug Prevention: Handbook Two

Additional copies available at www.milestogodrugeducation.com
Kelly Townsend, M.S. & Jonathan Scott

This book was developed from the Parent Meeting Lecture created by Miles To Go for their Drug Abuse Prevention Lecture Series. Miles To Go is based in Southern California.

The information contained in this book is meant to provide the reader with information for drug abuse prevention purposes only. It is not a substitute for medical advice, diagnosis or treatment. A medical professional should be contacted immediately in cases of substance abuse and possible overdose.

While the authors have made every effort to provide accurate contact information and internet addresses at the time of publication, neither the publisher nor the authors assume any responsibility for errors or changes that occur after publication.

ISBN: 1466354682

TABLE OF CONTENTS

Dedication

To all the moms (and dads) who realize they could use a little help and are proactive enough to go looking for it.

Special Dedication

We would like to dedicate this book to all our parents; those still with us and those who have passed on. Thank you for your efforts then; and thank you even more for your continued efforts. We couldn't have done this without you, and that's a fact.

Acknowledgements

We want to extend our heartfelt thanks to all our proofreaders— your dedication to the content when it is in its raw form goes beyond the call. Thanks also go out to the cover models—you guys look great!

Our Philosophy for This Book

Years ago, when we first considered writing our handbook series, we decided that most people have little or no desire to curl up with a cup of cocoa and a drug abuse prevention book. We did think, however, that moms and dads would grab a quick read and mark things off on a checklist. We wanted to create an easy to read, easy to use handbook that could expand its reach online as we added to the discussion and checklist on our website.

As we wrote, though, we soon realized that the scope of the information exceeded the parameters of what would normally be considered a handbook, and we decided it was more important to give you everything we had than it was to adhere to the original notion of preconceived volume size. We hope you will still carry it with you and read a section or two while you sit in carpool or at the soccer field.

This book is a checklist of all the little things we say and do; and it is an exploration of the power those little things have to shape our children's futures. How we talk to our kids, the patterns we establish in our lives, and the skills we teach and model have the capacity to keep our kids away from drugs and alcohol, out of addiction and rehab, free from sexually transmitted diseases and unwanted pregnancies, and less likely to end up in jail or an early grave. This is the second in our series of handbooks that are designed to provide parents and anyone working with young people the tools they need to keep kids safe in a world full of drugs.

A Note from the Authors

The concept for this book was created *by* a mother, but it is not just *for* mothers. Dads, grandparents, nannies, babysitters, counselors, teachers—anyone who cares for or about children—will benefit from the wisdom found in this handbook and checklist.

Introduction
Keep the Conversation Going

I wrote *The Mother's Checklist of Drug Prevention* lecture many years ago as a parenting presentation, so mothers could have a simple checklist of things they could do to lessen the chances their kids would use drugs and alcohol. It all started when, as a new mom, I became obsessed with every parenting book I could get my hands on. As I read, I chose the ideas that best fit my personality, my goals for my child, and my parenting style. As a drug educator with over 16 years in the classroom, I also paid particular attention to how each concept related to substance abuse prevention.

Over the years, as I gathered and applied these concepts in my roles as mom and teacher, I had the added pleasure of being able to compare notes with thousands of other parents who were as concerned as I was about keeping our kids safe and healthy. These ideas are condensed here for you in a checklist that includes parenting, communication, relationships, and skill building. Don't be misled by the fact that there is very little direct discussion about drugs—the core goal of the checklist is to make sure that drugs and alcohol never become issues.

When it comes to substance abuse, parents the world over want their kids to be protected, and yet there is no one thing that will keep young people safe. Every child is unique, and efforts to make one technique fit them all will certainly lead to frustration; and yet young people as a group have the same basic needs—they want to feel safe, loved, listened to, liked, capable and important. While there is no cookie cutter child, the items covered in the checklist will help build a proactive environment that allows children to build skills and resiliencies that will help them get what they need from the world without having to turn to drugs.

The ideas presented in the checklist have proved successful for a broad spectrum of parents and parenting professionals; the key is to start as early as you can and stay consistent in your efforts. As you start to apply the checklist concepts, you may also find they are not limited just to parenting, but can be applied in other areas of your work and social life as well.

This handbook is made up of all the elements I learned about in my research journey, but one of the most important is that families are most effective when they work together; so for the rest of this effort I want to add the input of Jonathan, the other half of our parenting team. From here on, the voice of this book will change from the "I" of Kelly to the "we" of Miles To Go. *September 2011*

How to Use This Handbook

Please Do Not Proceed Any Further Without Reading the Following Information!

This book is divided into 4 parts:

Part 1 answers some important questions we hear most often from parents.

Part 2 covers patterns of language that we use within our families. The nature of the language we use can shape our families positively or negatively; positive language will allow children to thrive and negative language will put them on the path to failure. Our goal is to encourage the use of positive proactive language when we communicate, thereby helping to decrease the potential for drug use inspired by frustration, stress, depression, anger, or anxiety.

Part 3 is about patterns of behavior we establish within our families. Positive patterns may be second nature to some parents, but many others struggle daily with negative patterns; a few parents don't even recognize they have patterns and spend their days wondering why the relationships in their families are so terribly unpleasant.

Part 4 is *Everything I Ever Learned About Parenting I Learned at Disneyland*. Part 4 covers, in a tongue in cheek way, practical ways to incorporate into our daily lives all the little things we can say and do to reduce stress and decrease the possibility of substance abuse.

In addition to the checklist, most sections include these recurring elements:

- **Keep in Mind** will highlight major issues to be discussed.
- **The Words We Use** will talk about and give examples of the language used when speaking with children.
- **Establish a Pattern** will suggest ways to practice and repeat the important ideas without becoming incredibly boring and one-dimensional.
- **Lessons Learned** will quickly recap what was just covered.
- **Links** will guide you to additional content on the Internet. All references are also cited so you can investigate these topics in more detail on your own.

Our goal is to make the checklist a living document that continues to grow via the use of social media such as Twitter (popular at the time of this writing in 2011), podcasting (such as iTunes), blogging (we currently use Blogger), and our website, which will have a page dedicated to this handbook and checklist.

A number of the concepts addressed in this book have come from parents who shared their stories with us over the years, and *The Mother's Checklist of Drug Prevention—Part 2* will grow out of the responses this book generates.

Used as intended, this checklist should be referred to throughout the year. It would be best if it were accessible every day, but at a minimum you should mark your calendar at least three times each year—e.g., January, May, and September—to remind yourself to pull out the checklist and spend a few minutes reviewing your thoughts. Then, as one of your New Year's resolutions, mark the next year's calendar and make a new copy of your checklist, so you can continue to hone your Ninja parenting skills.

Part 1

Answering the Big Questions

1.1 When Should We Start Talking About Drugs?

"Earlier than you might think, but not in the way you might think," could be an answer that inspires you to throw this book across the room, but please don't. In our complex, media-saturated world, our young children (as young as four) need and can handle drug information. That does not mean, however, they need all the information available. It used to be that parents could shield their children from information about drug use and alcohol abuse if they worked really hard at it, but today that effort would require an almost complete removal from the civilized world. Not only are kids using drugs and alcohol at increasingly earlier ages, they are also exposed to their existence and use via the various media at ever younger ages.

Barring a complete ban on all media, which would seriously hamper your children's ability to integrate into today's culture, it's pretty much impossible to shield them from images of and references to drugs and alcohol, even at incredibly tender ages. Cruella De Vil smokes cigarettes in *101 Dalmatians*, and Linguini gets drunk in *Ratatouille*—that doesn't mean we think these movies are bad for your children. (Seriously, did you already forget the title of Part 4?) It does mean that you should watch what your children watch, and discuss with them what you have seen. You want to avoid confusion and take advantage of the teachable moments these incidents provide.

It will pay great dividends if you are constantly scanning in your everyday life for opportunities that allow for discussions about drugs and alcohol. Be on the lookout for anti-drug ads on TV, and keep your eyes peeled for billboards with alcohol advertisements or anti-drug messages as you drive. If you can find a way to play off of the context of the moment, it will seem less like you're giving a lecture and more like you're having a conversation.

Even when your child presents you with what appears to be the prefect opportunity to talk, you have to be careful to not over-

1

answer. Our daughter recently asked a question about a drug, and as Kelly proceeded to tell her everything she thought was appropriate for her to know about the subject, the poor kid's eyes glazed over. She looked at Kelly and said, "No, mom, all I wanted to know was if it was a legal or illegal drug. I just heard it on the news." Try to find out what it is your child is actually asking for before you give them Wikipedia.

On the other hand, if your child asks a question you don't know the answer to, don't make stuff up; and certainly don't fall back on the old adages about fried brains. With as much information as we have on our website alone, there is no need to make things up and every reason to educate yourself a little each day, so you're not caught flat-footed every time you get a question.

You also have to constantly be mindful of the age and emotional resilience of the child you are speaking to at the moment. Every child will have a different comfort level, and every age group will have a limited range of what is an appropriate level of information. It is perfectly advisable, in our opinion, to discuss with your four-year-old child the notion that cigarettes are dangerous, unhealthy, smelly, pollution-spewing tubes of nastiness that cause your teeth to yellow and give you premature wrinkles. The age of four, however, is a little young to hear all the intricacies of how cancers invade and kill the bodies of smokers at a terrible rate. Little children think in very black and white terms, and if you go down the cancer road with them too soon, it may inspire a disproportionate fear that every person they see smoking is about to pitch over dead at any moment—right in front of them!

On the other hand, if someone in your family currently uses tobacco, you should take care to avoid trying to make your children feel better by misleading them about the dangers of tobacco. By doing so, you undermine the reality of the dangers posed by tobacco use. As drug educators with 16 years experience in teaching about the perils of tobacco, we regularly come across young students who challenge the notion that smoking is harmful, typically with an observation along the lines of, "My grandmother has smoked for 50 years, and her doctor says she's totally fine." Inaccurate statements about how tobacco affects human bodies might serve the purpose of making your children feel better for the moment, but the cost is

2

simply too great if that same misinformation increases the like, your children will smoke when they get older.

Further opportunities to discuss drugs will arise each time your children take medicine. Very young children should learn that medicine is not candy; that beneficial things can be bad for you if you don't follow dosage instructions; and that all problems are not immediately solved by taking a pill. Discussions about healthy lifestyles and non-medicinal solutions (e.g., a glass of water is often better than taking aspirin for dealing with a headache) can be added as you see fit.

So, look where we already find ourselves—ask one simple question, and a pool of quicksand immediately surrounds us! Yes, you should tell your four-year-old that tobacco is bad, but don't scare them too much. Answer their questions, but don't give too much information. Don't lie or mislead, but don't leave them thinking that Granny is going to die any minute now.

Our answer to the very first question posed in this handbook should give you deep insight into why we were moved to write it— the simplest things get complex really fast when it comes to how to talk to our kids about drugs and alcohol in an educational and age-appropriate way.

Parents are constantly confronted with the danger and confusion alcohol and drugs are so good at inspiring. A look at just a few of the issues we face in 2011 helps to define the challenge:

◆ Almost 90% of all smokers begin before the age of 19, and many start by age 13. You can't wait until middle school to talk to your kids about tobacco.

◆ Around the world, inhalant abuse in children begins well before the age of ten. Colored markers with scents like blueberry and lemon are OK to sniff, because they are water-based; but some dry erase markers can be toxic to your brain, heart, liver, kidneys, and bone marrow when the solvents they use are purposefully concentrated and inhaled. You can't wait until middle school to talk to your kids about inhalants.

◆ Numerous studies say that, on average, around 20% of all 8th graders have been drunk outside the presence of an adult. You can't wait until high school to talk to your children about alcohol.

♦ As of August 2011, 16 states allowed the use of medical marijuana, and Massachusetts was poised to become the 17th. In 2012, Californians will again vote on whether to legalize possession and use of small quantities of marijuana. Young people in our classes regularly admit a high level of confusion over what to think about marijuana. You can't wait until high school to talk about marijuana.

These examples represent the tiniest little sliver of what parents have to deal with today when it comes to drugs and alcohol. It's no wonder so many feel helpless when they try to guide their children down a safe path. Despair not, however. Instead, read on, and make your way to the checklist!

Lessons Learned: When to Start Talking

You can start talking about drugs earlier than you think. Information should be in context, age-appropriate, and truthful. Don't diminish negative consequences with misinformation—try to reassure without misleading. You don't have to tell them everything. Look for and take advantage of every opportunity to talk. Pick a subject and try to educate yourself a little each day.

Links: See links section 1A

Using the Checklist: When Should We Start Talking About Drugs?

☐ Have I started the conversation/Am I continuing the conversation?

☐ Do I appreciate my children's level of exposure to and awareness about drugs and alcohol?

☐ Am I checking to see if I understand what my child is actually asking?

☐ Am I educating myself a little each day?

☐ Am I misleading my children in the pursuit of comfort?

☐ Am I teaching my children about labels and dosages?

☐ Am I careful with my language concerning medicine?

☐ Did I discuss anti-drug ads that we may have seen together or can I arrange to find one to discuss?

☐ Did I find an opportunity to discuss a movie or TV show with drug or alcohol references in it?

☐ Did I find at least one time to talk about a healthy lifestyle for our family?

1.2   Why Do Kids Use Drugs?

For every child who has ever made the decision to use drugs or alcohol, there exists in that tragic moment a completely unique set of circumstances; genetics, emotional state, social status, life skills, family, self-image, media influence, stress level, age, friends, and school are only a few of the variables that can contribute to the decision to start using. With that many elements exerting their influence, it seems an impossible task to identify why kids start using drugs and alcohol, and it really is daunting if considered from that detailed perspective.

Despite the myriad reasons kids cite for doing drugs, one overriding cause comes up in almost every discussion about motivations for teen use: stress. Young people today are stressed on almost every level. They have to do well in school, they have to be popular, they have to participate in sports and extracurricular activities that look good on college applications, they have to navigate the minefield of puberty and its associated mood fluctuations, they have to keep their parents happy and off their backs, they may have to work because of family money problems, they may struggle with issues of romance, bullying, teasing, physical and mental health problems, divorce, trouble getting organized, faith, learning disabilities, sex, and on top of all this, they are supposed to get plenty of sleep—which they don't.

A text message received by the child of a friend summed it all up. Upon entering high school as a freshman, one of her friends entering her second year at the same school sent her the following: "Social life, good grades, sleep. Pick two. Welcome to high school." With all the stress young people are under today, they need a huge array of skills if they are to succeed. If they lack those skills, the challenges can be so great that drugs and alcohol start to look like very viable options. Unfortunately, those who do choose to deal with stress by doing drugs fail to understand one of the basic tenets of drug use by young people—it results in a net stress gain. In other words, the very thing they think will reduce the stress in their lives ends up contributing even more. The resulting feedback loop of stress/use/stress/use can cause them to spiral out of control very quickly.

No discussion of why teens choose to use drugs and alcohol can be complete unless it deals with the notion of peer pressure. As we said in our first book, *Not All Kids Do Drugs*, an understanding of peer pressure is fundamental if you want any insight into what it's like to be a teen, but many parents' notions of how peer pressure operates are inaccurate. Essentially, it is a part of the human condition to experience self-doubt, and teens, whether they show it or not, have more than their fair share of it. The desire to fit in, to be popular, and to validate their personal worth in the eyes of another are core concerns for most kids, and often they find it easiest to realize these goals if they conform to a particular group dynamic.

The typical adult model of peer pressure loses validity, however, when it assumes that the group, or at least one socially powerful member of the group, is actively insisting that the teen wishing to gain acceptance must behave in a specific way if they are to be welcomed into the fold. If only it were that simple. Yes, the teen must conform, but they must do so through trial and error as they attempt to figure out what it is that will win them acceptance. The pressure to experiment with behaviors that may or may not win favor is very likely to come from the mind of the one trying to gain admission to the group rather than from the group or its individual members. How they dress, how they speak, and how they act, including whether they drink and do drugs, all come into play as means of winning entry into the group.

Unfortunately, a large facet of the social scene for many teens is parties, and the majority of these parties include the use of drugs and alcohol. If a young person wants to fit in at a party, the quickest, easiest, most visible way to do so is to grab a drink or smoke a joint. Young people who lack a strong, positive self-image will often fall into this trap.

When we add in all the other reasons associated with drug and alcohol use by young people—boredom, rebellion, curiosity, the desire to relax and have a good time with friends—it's easy to see how some parents feel powerless when confronted with the challenge. All is not lost, however, for two very important reasons. First, for almost every reason cited as to why young people ultimately decide to start using drugs, there is a way to redefine what is happening in that instant. That redefining concept is the idea that drugs are really not the issue we're dealing with—drugs are just a symptom of another problem that isn't being dealt with in a better way. This concept leads us to the second important reason to not lose hope over the complexity of why kids use: almost every element listed has a corresponding action which, when taken when children are young, can insulate them from the effects of that risk. These two ideas—drugs aren't the problem, but are a symptom; and simple actions, taken when kids are young, can insulate them from drugs and alcohol—are the essence of the checklist.

Lessons Learned: Why Kids Use

Drug and alcohol use isn't the problem; it's a symptom of an underlying issue that isn't being dealt with effectively. Simple steps, taken consistently when kids are young, can inoculate them from choosing drugs and alcohol by giving them the skills and resiliencies they need to be effective and comfortable in their lives. Parents must be vigilant and aware, so they can accurately assess their children's developmental state and emotional well-being.

Links: See links section 1B

Using the Checklist: Why Do Kids Use Drugs?

☐ Are my children stressed by over-scheduling? What are my options if they are?

☐ Am I aware of the many forces that can cause stress in my children's lives?

☐ Do I have an accurate picture of who my children are and what their strengths and weaknesses are?

☐ Do I have a plan that focuses on my children's strengths and helps them where they are struggling?

☐ Do my children have the social skills and self-confidence required for success?

☐ Are my children struggling to fit in? Are they making unhealthy decisions in order to be popular?

☐ Do my children have some down time?

☐ Is everyone getting enough sleep? How can I improve this situation if they aren't?

☐ Is my child a follower or a leader?

☐ Am I making time in my busy life to pay enough attention to my children?

Part 2

Life is a Series of Conversations

2.1   How High Do You Float When You Get High?

While this may be one of the funniest and most innocent questions we've ever been asked, it points out a huge concern—younger kids are almost universally confused about drugs and alcohol. They are hampered by literal thinking, baffled by slang and figures of speech, and incapable of conceiving why anyone would want to take drugs. Also, a lot of parents we speak with have trouble differentiating between children being aware of something and their actually understanding it. Most kids have seen someone who is drunk, be it in person or by seeing it portrayed in a television show or movie, and yet most of them have no idea how it came about, what it feels like to the person experiencing it, and what negative impacts may be associated with it both immediately and over time. Nobody likes to be seen as ignorant, and young people are no exception. Many times they will feign understanding in order to deflect criticism. We have to keep this in mind when we speak to our children about drugs and alcohol, and constantly check for understanding as our conversations progress.

Keep in Mind: Kids often lack a detailed understanding of even the most basic drug terms, definitions, and concepts. Although they may frequently use a term (e.g. "He's *addicted* to video games."), they lack any meaningful understanding of that term. Think of drug education as being a little like math—if you don't have an understanding of the basics, there is very little chance you will work well with the more advanced concepts that come later. Drug education exposes young people to a huge amount of new information; and confusion, while completely predictable and normal, can be lessened by discussing with your children what they think they heard, comparing it to what you think is true, finding out what is actually true, and gently correcting any misconceptions.

10

The Words We Use: Student Questions

The questions our students ask us can provide a little insight into what the average level of drug understanding is for older elementary and younger middle school students (4th-6th grade), but it is often the students' assumptions that follow the answers to these questions that give a deeper appreciation for the misconceptions even the simplest drug and alcohol discussions can inspire. A good example:

We say, "Coffee has the drug caffeine in it."
Student response, "Coffee is a drug!?!"
We explain, "Coffee is a beverage, but it does have the drug caffeine in it."
Student response, "But it's not really a drug. You can't get addicted to coffee."
We continue, "If you drink enough of it over a long enough period of time, you can get addicted to the caffeine in coffee, but just because you drink coffee doesn't mean you're addicted to it."
Student immediately jumps to, "So you're saying my mom is addicted to drugs!?"
We explain, "No, I didn't say that at all. I don't even know your mom."

This exchange, while obviously not the same every time, is a very accurate representation of how confused kids can get over the simplest drug concepts. As we have said, young people think in very black and white terms, and that can take conversations off track very quickly. The preceding dialogue highlights a few of the possible misunderstandings adults must be aware of when talking about drugs and alcohol with their children. Take a minute to appreciate the progression of alarming misperceptions that come about in a kid's mind as they mix previous confusions with new, misunderstood facts.

- First, almost every young kid we've ever met will immediately tell you, "Drugs are bad."

- So, "Drugs are bad, but my parents don't do bad things, so they must not do drugs."

11

- Then they hear coffee has a drug in it, so we move to, "My parents drink coffee, but they don't do drugs, so coffee can't really have a drug in it."

- Once they realize that coffee does indeed have the drug caffeine in it, we get, "Drugs are addictive, and coffee has a drug in it, and so my parents must be drug addicts."

- From there, it's just a short leap to, "Drug addicts die, so my parents are going to die because they drink coffee."

Before we know it, we have a fifth grader crying as her mother pulls into the drive-thru for a cup of fresh-brewed goodness. We now officially have a problem, and we have a parent who wants to know, "What the hell have you been telling my kid!" As you can see, this can be difficult, and we're the professionals! Imagine how fast the descent into chaos can be for parents trying to have a drug conversation with their children.

This is not in any way intended to discourage you from having conversations with your children, and it is certainly not an attempt to get you to stop drinking coffee. It is simply an effort to point out how important it is to educate yourself a little each day, and to constantly strive to understand and to be understood when you are communicating with your children. That is a skill that can be learned, and once learned it can be honed to a fine edge. Once it is, a great thing becomes possible—you can communicate effectively with your kids. You might even be able to keep a straight face if you ever have to face the question Kelly got from a sixth grade student in 2010, "What other drugs besides alcohol can you snort up your nose?"

Lessons Learned: How We Teach

We have a few policies that help us avoid leaving students baffled and afraid. With a few tweaks, they may help you, too.

Our policy: We deliver information that is age-appropriate and accepted as accurate by the greater medical and scientific community.

When you speak to your family: You know your children better than anyone. Trust your gut instinct as to whether your children are ready for a particular topic. That said; don't trust that part of you that wants to keep your children innocent and safe from the world forever. Your babies will always grow up faster than you want them to, and you need to protect them by teaching them about drugs and equipping them with skills, not by keeping them in the dark.

Our policy: We start at the beginning, by discussing where the drug comes from (plant, animal, chemical process); how it was originally used; its place in society, medicine, religion, tribal ritual, etc; what parts of the body it affects; that it can have good and bad attributes according to how, where, why and by whom it is used; and possibly any slang or specific terminology that may apply to it. Older students need to hear about how the drug might impact their lives and the lives of their friends if they get involved with it, and they need to hear about how to engineer their lives so they can avoid drugs and alcohol.

When you speak to your family: You don't have to be drug experts, but you can educate yourself a little each day so as not to appear completely lost. More importantly, though, you can tell your children how you feel about drug and alcohol use by young people. You can talk about your fears, and your hopes, and you can tell your children you will do anything to keep them safe, even if they might not like it so much when you do it. In other words, you can teach your children your values and show them through your actions that you have character. That is so much more powerful than anything we could ever do.

Our policy: We are pretty adamant that our students are to learn about drugs from us, not from each other, especially when they are younger. Yes, there's lots of science out there that says kids can learn very effectively from each other, but only after their information has been vetted for accuracy. As you have seen from the material earlier in this section, accuracy is not one of the strong suits for young people when it comes to drug and alcohol information.

When you speak to your family: You may not be your children's primary source of accurate drug and alcohol information yet, but you are definitely who your children look to for guidance. You can avoid a lot of heartache if you don't let their friends be the only voice in their heads.

Our policy: Every time a student asks a question or makes a statement, we strive to understand what exactly is being said before we respond. If we misunderstand the question, our answer will do nothing but sow confusion.

When you speak to your family: You can do exactly the same thing.

Using the Checklist: How High Do You Float When You Get High?

☐ Am I conscious of the confusion drug and alcohol discussions can cause, both for me and my children?

☐ Do I know the difference between awareness and understanding?

☐ Do I check for understanding when I speak with my children? (Reiterate what the speaker has said to be sure both parties are on the same page.)

☐ Do I know that there is no tobacco in Tabasco?

☐ Have I tried to educate myself about drugs and alcohol recently?

2.2   What Are Positive Proactive Patterns of Language and Communication?

There are entire courses taught on patterns of communication in families. One of the most influential authors on this subject, Deborah Tannen, Ph.D, a professor of Linguistics at Georgetown University, opened her book *You Just Don't Understand: Women and Men in Conversation* with the sentence, "Each person's life is lived as a series of conversations."

Much of this handbook is dedicated to the idea that the way we converse with our children can literally lead them toward or away from substance use. Properly directed conversations can establish patterns of language that help your children communicate effectively. Effective communication acts directly to reduce one of the major reasons cited for using drugs and alcohol—stress.

2.3   What is Positive Proactive Language?

Since it is the essence of what the entire second section is focused on, let's start with the basics and define the term Positive Proactive Language. According to Miriam Webster, the three parts break down into:

Positive: marked by optimism (as in, "a positive point of view"), having a good effect (as in, "a positive role model), assured, confident;

Proactive: acting in anticipation of future problems, needs or changes;

Language: the words, their pronunciation, and the methods of combining them when used and understood by a community.

So, with positive proactive language we have a means of communicating that is marked by its optimism and its commitment to creating an action as opposed to responding to one. This will be the pattern of language we will reference any time we are discussing effective communication, and it is the pattern of language that has the power to shape the skills and resiliencies our children need to realize their full potential and avoid the pitfalls of drug and alcohol use. As parents, our goal is to inspire our children to be independent thinkers, but we want them to be safe at the same time. We don't want them to be overly praised, self indulgent, dependent children who can't make a move without us. To keep them safe, we must instill a sense of strength, self-esteem and responsibility in them as they grow. The way we speak to them is an important part of reaching these goals.

If you are motivated to explore more about how to lead a proactive life, we encourage you to look into the work of Steven Covey, who lists "Be Proactive" as Habit 1 in his groundbreaking book, *The 7 Habits of Highly Effective People*. Granted, his work does not qualify for the "easy to read" or "handbook" categories, but it is one of those rare writings that can change lives. Only you can decide if you want to do that kind of work, but if you do, it will definitely make you "proactive." With over five million books in print in 32 languages, you won't have to work very hard to get a copy.

Be mindful that positive proactive language is not the same as psychobabble. The goal here is not to add confusion via the use of terms only a PhD would understand. Kelly recently witnessed a father dropping off a carload of young boys who appeared to be about six years old. Because they weren't paying attention to what they were doing or to the risk of cars driving past, the father admonished them to be more careful by saying, "Boys! Are you being situationally aware here?!" Really? With six-year-olds? "Situational awareness" is a term pilots use for being present in the environment that surrounds them. The only person lacking in situational awareness that day was the dad—six-year-olds don't process language that complex. Positive proactive language does not necessarily mean complex language.

Keep in Mind: Remember our mantra: reducing substance use by young people has very little to do with knowing a lot about drugs. One of the biggest agents of change is using and teaching positive proactive language. The pattern of communication we set up with our young children plays a powerful role in the relationships we build with them, how they respond to us, their perceptions about their lives and futures, how they relate to their friends and social influences, and the belief that they are in large part the masters of their own destiny.

Establish a Pattern: Repetition

We encourage you to start setting up positive proactive language patterns in your daily life. Begin establishing language patterns as early as possible, because the parents who do this have the most success and influence as their children become teenagers and college students.

2.4   Proactive Speech

Keep in Mind: When you use positive proactive speech, you show your children that you are doing your best to create situations as opposed to blindly reacting to them as they occur. By teaching your children to change "can't" language into "can" language, you help them to shade situations positively and to expect positive outcomes versus negative. When your children see they can exert control over how they see situations, it gives them a sense of power and confidence; and this sense of self-direction can come into play when they need to deal with offers of drugs and alcohol at parties. When they learn to view situations as changeable and controllable, rather than preordained, and to see that there are always multiple options on how to deal with any given situation, they gain the confidence to be the authors of their personal stories.

The Words We Use: Language Influences Perception

Our language influences how we view situations and their impact.

Language checks: Take a moment to reflect on your daily language style. Which one are you?

◆   "I can do this," or, "I'm not sure I can do this."

- "I can do a cartwheel, if I just practice enough," or, "I tried it once, and I fell. I can't do cartwheels."
- "I can make this work," or, "I don't think this will work."
- "Let's look at all the options," (Kelly's favorite phrase) or, "I have to do it this way. This is the way I've always done it."
- "I can add and subtract, but I'll need help if I want to get better at multiplication and long division," or, "I'm just not good at math."
- "If we work hard, prioritize, plan, and save, we can go on the vacation we want," or, "We could never afford a cruise like that."
- "I can stop biting my fingernails. I've got to commit to catching myself in the act and deciding that isn't what I want," or, "I think I read one time that fingernail biting is genetic. You can't change what is."
- "Smoking is an addiction, and it will be hard to stop at first, but other people have done it, so I can do it too!" or, "I always fail when I try to quit. I must have an addictive personality."

2.5   Reactive Speech

Keep in Mind: Reactive language is much more than just saying, "I can't," in any given situation; it is the innate sense that you are powerless over that situation and nothing you do will change the outcome. It is not only the language of victimization and persecution, but also the language of absolutes—like "you always" and "you never" statements. Many times, reactive language patterns form when people feel the need to be absolved of responsibility—the overriding sense of, "It's not my fault, it was (anything external: my boss, my wife, my kids, my job, my mom, my dad…)."

When parents use reactive language, they not only teach their children to expect failure and add unnecessary drama and turmoil to their lives, they also teach them to avoid responsibility for and ownership of their actions. Martin Seligman, a self-proclaimed pessimist and author of *The Optimistic Child*, says "Pessimists' reactions to adversity are often overblown and exaggerated." With their infectious absolutism, they create families full of frustration and defeat.

Upon reflection, many of us may find that we are reflexively reactive, in that we do it automatically as a response to any perceived threat, real or imagined. If your spouse says something like, "Wow, there really are a lot of dirty dishes tonight," and your immediate response, be it verbal or mental, is, "I didn't dirty them all! I was really busy today. How was I supposed to get them washed?" you may have a problem with automatic reactivity. There probably wasn't a half-ton of passive aggression in your spouse's comment, it was just an observation. The threat was in what you read into the comment; and the fact that your reaction occurred so rapidly and automatically would indicate that you were trained to be reactive a long time ago. Now, it's your default setting—it's just the way you see things. Working toward a more positive, proactive read on communication requires that you first be able to recognize reactivity, both in what it feels like and what it sounds like. If you don't, there's a high likelihood you are training your children to be just like the reactive you.

The Words We Use: Reactive Language

Reactive language doesn't just create a climate of expected failure; it also leads to blame and feelings of powerlessness.

Language checks—do you ever find yourself saying things like:

◆ "Why don't you ever listen?"
◆ "You always… (Fill in the blank.)"
◆ "There's nothing I can do about it. That's just the way I am."
◆ "I'd like to, but I just don't have the time."
◆ "I'm too old to get a college degree. That ship has sailed."
◆ "That's just the way boys/girls are."
◆ "Why do you always blame me?"
◆ "Why do you always make such a mess?"
◆ "All kids are going to drink alcohol sooner or later."

Reactive language is more than just a pattern of speech; it is a world view which, unfortunately, is self-fulfilling. If parents believe that all kids will drink, their kids get the message, "We expect this of you," and they will drink much more frequently than children of parents who have made it clear they expect their children to abstain.

As an example of reactive speech, we'll use a family friend who finds herself trapped by a four-year-old with a drinking problem. The problem? She constantly laments, "I can't get my son to drink anything but juice. He won't drink water or milk." When he was really little, she was even reduced to giving him a bottle full of juice at bedtime, because "it was the only way to get him to go to sleep."

The first thing that has to happen if this situation is to change is for her to realize that the main reason he won't drink anything but juice is that she continues to give it to him. If she didn't give it to him, he wouldn't be able to drink it. The crux of the issue is this: she isn't able to deal with the way her son acts when she doesn't give him the juice he has come to expect. She has lost control and views herself as a victim, and she reinforces this with the amazingly powerful words, "I can't…" and "He won't…"

You might be justified in wondering why this is a big deal. Who has the time or energy to fight with a kid about juice? Unfortunately, his juice habit was cited by their family dentist as one of the main causes of about $3,000 worth of dental work her son recently had to have done. The bigger issue, though, is that she is setting up a dynamic which will affect how she and her son relate to and communicate with each other over decades, not days, in situations where much bigger issues than juice will have to be dealt with.

So how can she go about changing the juice consumption in her home? First, she has to decide to take ownership of the situation. Next, she has to look at it from a new perspective and trust that change will occur if given a chance. Last, she has to be willing to suffer a modicum of upset while the transition away from juice is underway.

There are a couple of ways this could go. The first would be to just go cold turkey on the juice. The primary drive in all human beings, and that includes even four-year-olds, is survival. Given the new reality of no juice, her son would eventually be driven by sheer thirst to drink something else; but she may be driven to insanity in the interim.

A better solution would be to change the list of drink options her son has to choose from. "We are all out of juice. What would you like instead? We have milk, or water, or how about some water with bubbles in it?" Now, kids are smart, and past experience has shown her son that if he screams loudly enough, he'll get what he wants; but the only reason he knows that to be true is that, in the past, she has always given in. For that to change, she has to change. Maybe she has to get a little more creative if she wants things to go more smoothly.

Kids will usually be more amenable to a change if they feel they have had a hand in the decision. Perhaps the afternoon before she offered milk instead of juice, she could have engaged her son in the making of chocolate milk ice cubes. That evening, her son could put two of "his" ice cubes in his milk. Obviously, the goal here isn't to substitute one sugary drink for another, but a few ice cubes bobbing in a glass of milk is still very different from a glass full of juice.

Maybe she could buy a few ice cube trays that make cool shapes—Mickey Mouse is big in our house. Colored ice cubes and a few slices of fruit can go a long way toward making sparkling water more palatable to a picky drinker. Maybe the change could be hastened along by a special cup that he gets to decorate with all his favorite characters. Bendy straws with about a dozen loops in them also have the power to distract young drinkers from what is actually being drunk through them.

The big issue here is that the son's drinking habits have to change, but so do the mother's habits as the drink provider. Ultimately, change will happen when she decides to care enough about the situation to do something about it; but often the first thing that has to change is for the person to realize they have the power to bring it about. The real change, though, is more basic—Mom has to change her language from, "I can't…" to, "I can…", thereby living up to the positive in positive proactive speech, and from, "He won't…" to, "He will, if I…", which fulfills the proactive requirement of causing an action rather than being the victim of one. This is the essence of positive proactive language versus reactive language, and it is also its power.

Lessons Learned: Positive Proactive Language

- Positive proactive language makes for healthy communication and encourages responsibility; reactive language creates an atmosphere of powerlessness, failure, and blame.
- Seemingly small things when your kids are young become big things as they get older—patterns are powerful.
- You may have been deeply conditioned to be reactive, but you can change with awareness and effort.
- Perspective is everything. The same situation can be seen as controllable or controlling.
- Find another way to say it, and you can create a new way to do it!
- You model positive proactive language for your children. They will behave much the way you do.
- Reactive parents are always trying to appease their children, adhere to their impossible schedules, and survive their manic lives; they have a feeling of being out of control.
- Proactive parents are ready for the curve balls that life throws them, in that they are flexible and open to new ways of getting the job done.

Links: See links section 2A

Using the Checklist: Positive Proactive Language

☐ Do I recognize positive proactive speech when I speak it or hear it?

☐ Can I identify patterns of communication that I already have, and group them into positive and negative language? Am I more positive and proactive, or am I more reactive?

☐ Am I using positive and proactive language with myself?

☐ Am I doing the same with my spouse, others, and especially my children?

☐ Am I mindful of the way my words are interpreted by others?

☐ Am I setting an example of success with the language I use with my children?

Using the Checklist: Negative Reactive Language

☐ Am I monitoring my speech and eliminating negative and reactive language?

☐ Am I careful about using absolutes, like "all," "never," and "always?"

☐ Am I sensitive to absolute statements like, "All kids are going to drink eventually," and the chance that they will become self-fulfilling prophesies?

☐ Am I recognizing negative and reactive language in my thoughts?

☐ Am I recognizing it in others?

☐ Are my reactions overblown or exaggerated?

☐ Am I trying to stop pessimistic thinking and language?

☐ Am I being careful about labeling my child?

☐ Am I responding to my children, or am I reacting to them?

2.6   Establishing Proactive Problem Solving

Keep in Mind: A big part of living a positive proactive life is the ability to problem solve. If you can define and verbalize problems in your life, you have taken the first step toward resolving any issue. Often, the first step is the hardest—identifying exactly what the problem is. Once you define the problem, you can move on to exploring and applying options in an effort to achieve resolution. Problem solving can be simply laid out in the pattern: **identify, try/apply,** and **resolve/try again.**

As parents, we can model problem-solving techniques for our children if we go through the process aloud. With time, practice, and repetition, it will become second nature for our children to employ these steps when faced with a challenge, and eventually this will become an integral part of their internal pattern of speech.

The Words We Use: How Do We Solve Problems?

Identify: "What is the challenge I face?"
Identify: "What are my options?"
Try/apply: "Here's what I'm going to do."
Resolve/try again: "Did it work? If yes—great! If not, what's next on my list of options?"

For a lot of kids, problem solving is not a part of the pre-loaded software package when we take them out of the box. Many don't even realize they have the power to do something about a problem they are faced with. By modeling this process, you empower your kids to make their lives better on their own, and you reduce the level of frustration in their lives. They should see you verbalize this process as you apply it in your life.

Verbalize the process: What's for dinner?

Most young kids have no concept of how much effort and planning goes into putting food on the table. One of the main reasons for this ignorance is that we work through the tasks of meal planning and preparation in our heads, not aloud. By doing it aloud, with our children present, we can increase awareness and teach problem

24

solving at the same time. It's even better if you solicit their participation in making the decisions about what to make and helping you prepare it as well.

Identify: "I need to get something ready for dinner, but everyone is coming home at different times tonight, so one sit-down meal won't do." **You've identified the issue.**

Identify: "We've got everything to make a big salad loaded with veggies, plus there's bread and soup. We can make the salad now, and everyone can heat their soup and bread when they're ready to eat." **You've explored your options and chosen a path.**

Try/apply: With your children's help, prepare the salad, lay out the plates, bowls, and silverware. **You've applied your solution.**

Resolve/try again: Everyone is fed a decent meal despite difficult circumstances.

PS: Each person is in charge of washing his or her dishes too!

Lessons Learned: Problem Solving

◆ Even very young children can understand that proactive problem solving begins with recognizing and verbalizing the problem.
◆ Engaging your kids in exploring and employing options allows them to practice and develop skills.
◆ The ability to problem solve will reduce frustration in your children's lives.

Using the Checklist: Problem Solving

☐ Am I verbalizing **identify, try/apply, resolve** problem solving techniques with my children regularly?

☐ Am I engaging my children in problem solving efforts regularly?

2.7 Establishing Patterns of Repetition

Keep in Mind: One way to problem solve and instill confidence is to use verbal repetition as a way to set up a pattern of language.

The Words We Use: "Is there any blood?" "Take a deep breath." "Let's look at all the options."

If you can establish a pattern that teaches your children effective strategies to deal with life's regular upsets, they will eventually learn to deal with common situations on their own. One of the most predictable events in children's lives is physical injury. Their response to an injury is often predicated on who is watching at the time of the injury. We've all witnessed a kid who suffers some sort of blow and then remains completely stoic until he has the attention of his mother, whereupon he lapses into complete hysterics. Often, minutes have passed between the physical insult and the teary response. While all of this is normal and expected, how we respond to the tears will set the stage for future situations.

Over the years, our immediate response to minor injuries, such as falls or bumps, is to ask, "Is there any blood?" This is done in a concerned but lighthearted manner—one that indicates that, while we understand the upset, we need to put it in perspective. Of course we would respond differently to a serious injury, but that is not the norm.

Another thing we do every time there are tears, whether they are injury-based or otherwise, is to say, "Take a deep breath." Deep breathing does wonders for human bodies—it reduces stress and focuses the mind. It can also serve to draw attention away from the injury and direct it to another area, in this case the purposeful in-and-out of controlled breathing. If you do this every time, a pattern develops. It's pretty amazing to see a child automatically start to purposefully breathe in the face of an injury or upset.

Another pattern Kelly is seriously committed to is, when confronted with a dilemma, to say, "Let's look at all our options." Jonathan is much more inclined to do the first thing that comes to mind, which, while very efficient in the short term, is usually dead wrong—and that, of course, means it is totally inefficient. Our child is obviously smarter than her dad, since she recently, when

26

confronted with a challenge, was heard to say, "Let me think about all my options here." Kelly literally had tears in her eyes! Jonathan, upon seeing Kelly's tears, said, "Take a deep breath."

Establish a Pattern: "I'm crying because…"

Identifying the "why" of children's upsets is a critical skill that can be developed at a very young age. As they gain insight through repetition, they are more quickly and effectively able to communicate to their parents what's wrong, thereby making a solution easier to implement. Even if children are too young to get more than gibberish out as the reason for upset, "I'm crying because…" is a pattern that will bear fruit for years to come if you can start to employ it early. At two, you're not going to get a lot of meaningful information, but by three you may get, "I'm crying because I fell," something you can understand and remedy.

As your children get older, the repetition of the pattern will allow a quick appraisal of the reason for the upset, and then you can either solve the dilemma or help your children solve the problem on their own. By elementary school, it may be, "I'm upset because my friend said something mean to me today." That opens the door to have a conversation about the stormy phases some friendships can go through, and how to keep momentary upsets in perspective.

In middle school, you may get, "I'm very disappointed in my grade, and I don't know how to fix it. I worked really hard!" A conversation about how to approach a teacher for extra help can give your child the confidence needed to keep trying in the face of adversity.

When your children reach high school, all your hard work will start to pay off, because you have shown yourself to be a good communicator and a good listener. Sometimes, as your children get older, listening will be much more important than actively participating in the solution. Your children will probably be pretty good at the solution side of the equation by then; your job will be to play the part of the sounding board as they explore their various options. Teenagers' lives can get pretty complicated, and having you to bounce ideas and concerns off of will go a long way as they navigate the difficult decisions about attending parties where drugs and alcohol will probably be present.

"I'm crying because..." opens up a world of discussions that can last a lifetime. If your children are already in middle or high school as you are reading this, it's not too late to begin a more mature pattern of dialogue with your children, but it does mean it will probably be more frustrating. It's never too late to show your kids you care, no matter how many times they tell you that you don't understand. Keep trying to find the words to help them fill in the blanks.

Lessons Learned: Establishing Patterns of Language

- Using the same pattern over and over will give your children a means of communicating their feelings and needs in a familiar, comfortable format.
- Listening is as important as offering solutions when your children are young, and grows more and more important as they grow older.

Using the Checklist: Patterns of Repetition

☐ Have I created a repetitive dialogue framework to use when my child is hurt or upset?

☐ Am I remembering to employ my key phrases when necessary?

☐ Am I really listening when my children tell me why they are crying?

2.8   Struggle

Keep in Mind: An important aspect of raising children that most parents instinctively work against is teaching kids how to struggle when they face problems. When we help our children overcome a problem or a challenge, we feel useful and good about ourselves. Unfortunately, we also build a dependency that will eventually harm the very children we intended to help, by stealing opportunities where they can develop the skills needed to successfully deal with future challenges.

The Words We Use: "Let mommy help you with that."

As parents, many of us have great difficulty standing on the sidelines as our kids wrestle with even the simplest problems. In the interest of saving time or making life easier for them, or us, we take over a job even when we haven't been asked to or when it is unnecessary. The simple act of reaching over to help children straighten their socks—because you feel as though you'll never make it out the door if you don't—is just one of a million examples of things we are guilty of doing in the interest of saving time.

When you take a task away from your children by doing it for them, you are establishing a destructive pattern. Those little tasks will then become the big tasks. Now you're running back home to retrieve the homework assignment your child forgot, or taking over their science projects because your skills at building scale models of the universe are more advanced than your children's are. Unfortunately, every time you save them or take over a task they could have done on their own, you take a little piece of their development away.

You don't have to make your children struggle with every job every time, but keep in the back of your mind the notion that they need to get over some of the hurdles by themselves. When they accomplish a task by themselves, they learn; and learning builds connections in their brains, sharpens their coordination, and helps create children who are more confident and independent.

Establish a Pattern: Using the Pro/Con List

A common issue young children struggle with is choosing which path to take, which option to exercise. A wonderful tool to aid in the process is the pro/con list. Whatever the issue, have your children divide a piece of paper or a Word document into vertical halves, and label one side "Pro" and one side "Con." Write all the reasons for a particular choice as your pro items, all the reasons against on the con side, and then have your children try to weigh the respective rewards of the items on one side as compared to the costs of the items on the other. This process can be especially helpful to the children who are predominantly visual learners, who need to see it before they can grasp it.

This is obviously a learned skill, and many children don't take to it willingly at first. You should fully expect to get a bushel full of, "I don't know," and at least one, "But I can't think of anything," per minute, but guide your children through the first few efforts. After the results of a choice are realized, take the time to go back and review your pro/con list to see if it was complete enough to have been an aid, or whether it needed more information to be helpful. Either way, you will be teaching your children to consider their options before making a decision, and that is a valuable skill they can employ in their struggle to make good choices.

Lessons Learned: Struggle

It is just as important for kids to learn how to fail as it is for them to learn how to succeed. There is no such thing as a world without failure, so it's important that children learn to put it in perspective. One of our favorite scenes in the movie *Meet the Robinsons* happens when the entire Robinson family has a passionate celebration of failure. If you never fail, all it means is that you never really tried.

◆ The right amount of challenge at the right time will make your children stronger.
◆ Over-protecting your children doesn't protect them in the long run.
◆ Balancing when to help and when to let your children struggle is very difficult, but try to err on the side of letting them struggle more than your heart tells you to—your heart is a wimp.

◆ Failure and struggle, when they aren't constant or thematic, are educational.

Using the Checklist: Struggle

☐ Am I allowing my children the opportunity to struggle?

☐ Do I encourage my children to try again when their first attempt isn't successful?

☐ Have I modeled graceful failure/lessons learned/trying again recently?

☐ Have I shown my children how to use a pro/con list?

☐ Am I sensitive to the level of frustration my children can manage before they melt down? What can I do to increase their coping skills?

2.9 Self-Talk

Keep in Mind: Self-talk, also referred to as inner speech or internal dialogue, is that swirling mix of positive and negative language that seems to constantly ramble on inside our heads. It can be so mundane as to prattle on for 20 minutes about whether or not to have another cookie, or so profound as to ponder one's value in the world. Dr. Shad Helmstetter, who has spent his career writing about, researching, and running programs on how to reverse negative inner speech, has determined that 77% of all self-talk is negative. His research indicates that most of us have a lot of work to do identifying, analyzing, and correcting the overwhelming river of negativity that runs through our heads on a daily basis.

The Process: Russian psychologist Lev Vygotsky's book *Thought and Language*, first published in English in 1962, is considered an essential work for understanding inner speech. While we can't do justice to the incredible complexity of his findings here, his basic premise is that children learn language from the external verbalization of their parents and others. From this spoken language of their parents, children move to problem solving and self-direction by thinking aloud, and then eventually to a completely silent and private inner speech, which is used to direct behavior, problem solve, and add meaning to thought. The way your children end up speaking to themselves with their silent inner voices—how they give meaning to their deepest interpretations of emotion and perception and self-worth—is based on the internal dialogue they develop from the words you use around them as they learn language.

The Words We Use: "I can do it, Mom!"

It is important to understand the difference between thought and inner speech. Young children seem to be thinking all the time—how else would so many different household items end up in toilets if their minds weren't constantly churning? Nevertheless, all thought is not inner speech—a toddler will draw on a wall all day long, but they don't wonder if their work is "good enough." It isn't until later, around the time they head off to school, that they start to speak silently and internally to themselves about thoughts of self-worth.

As we said just a moment ago, inner speech doesn't seem to occur at very young ages, but you can encourage positive speech patterns for your children when they are very young. This model, this positive style of external verbalization we spoke about, is what your children will base their language development upon. Later, when they start their silent, internal dialogue, the language they use to build it will be a language of positivity. Healthy, positive speech can teach your children how to cope, problem solve, and build their confidence. We have tried very hard to present examples of positive speech when we speak with our daughter. By the time she was seven, she had adopted the outlook of, "I can do it, Mom."

It should be noted that this is not a way to immediately fix perceived problems you may have with your children. Some estimates say that about 60% of your children's personalities are genetically driven, and those things won't change just because you speak in a certain way. Even though we did our best to model positive speech for our daughter, she still struggled mightily to overcome her fear of downhill slopes when she was learning how to ride her bike. Her fear in those situations was very real, and even though it seemed to us unnecessary and out of proportion to the size of the little bump she was about to coast down, no amount of, "You can do it!" calmed her fears.

What positive speech did do, however, was give her the tools she needed to work through her thoughts and feelings with the confidence that she can do what she puts her mind to. Compare that to children who have been branded "chicken" by parents frustrated with their children's timidity, and it is obvious that positive speech does more to build a resilient child than negative speech does.

The situation above is a very simplistic example, but by having your kids practice positive words at home and out in the world you train them to speak that way when they conduct inner dialogues. Later in life—when they are tasked with making decisions on their own—the self- esteem, self-monitoring, and self-regulating skills associated with positive inner speech will kick in to help direct their choices toward the safe and healthy and away from the impulsive and destructive.

Establish a Pattern: "I am."

♦ Maria Shriver has said that her dad always told her, "Everyone in the room is lucky to have you enter it." She says this built her confidence, and she has never forgotten it. We won't forget it either, because that simple act—positively reinforcing your children—pays such huge dividends later.

In his book *Parent Talk*, Chick Moorman wrote about "I am's," where he states that developing self-esteem in childhood is a quality-of-life issue as important as IQ. Moorman teaches that "I am's" are core beliefs that children hold about themselves. They are statements that children can make about themselves such as, "I am capable," "I am creative," or, "I am responsible." Used negatively, they become the destructive, "I am fat," and, "I am ugly."

Obviously, the tone of these "I am's" will identify the type of inner speech being used, and whether it is to the children's benefit or detriment. Children guided to regard themselves positively at an early age will carry that image in the tone of their inner speech for the rest of their lives. We have to be cautious here to not simply create children who have such a blind regard for their worth that they cannot conceive of a world that doesn't value them just because they exist—there is a huge difference between value and respect. All children have value, not all of them act in such a way as to earn respect—we earn the respect of others through hard work, honesty, and our spirit of charity, and it's important to differentiate between the two when we speak to our children on the topic of their worth.

Establish a Pattern: Self-Talk as We Age

The goal we have as we try to create a climate in which positive inner speech can flourish is to build in our children the confidence to be leaders rather than followers; to raise children who can choose what they want in any given situation rather than blindly follow in the path of a peer who might appear to be more popular at that moment. Confident children don't need to make choices that go against their beliefs in order to win the favor of a peer group; they aren't finding self-worth by pleasing others. Children awash in negative inner speech, however, are forced to seek worth in the eyes

34

of others, and they are often the ones who say yes to behaviors they know are unhealthy and destructive in the vain hope that they will win some degree of favor if they just acquiesce to the group's demands.

It pays to remember how powerful the forces of group acceptance are for teenagers. Take a moment to reflect back—can you remember an instance when someone said something to you when you were young that was so hurtful that you still carry it with you today? Why do other people's assessments of us carry such power? Maybe it's because, deep down, some of us agree with their opinions; it's what we've been saying about ourselves in our inner speech for years.

This can change, but for that to happen we must first realize the patterns of speech we currently employ. It takes a conscious choice to challenge the validity of negative self-talk—to get rid of that nasty, self-deprecating voice and replace it with one that isn't constantly dragging you through the dirt. If we don't take the time and effort to change it, though, what chance do our children have of growing up in a climate conducive to creating a positive inner voice?

Also, if we start modeling positive speech when our children are young, they have the potential to create a system of positive inner speech as they enter their teens. If we wait until they're older, we run the distinct risk that they will be overpowered by the messages constantly bombarding them via the various media. Mary Pipher, author of *Reviving Ophelia*, insists that we couldn't do more damage to our daughters with the images projected at them through the media if we tried. If our children are led to believe at a very young age that they are members of an inferior group, the battle for self-esteem is made more difficult when we enter it later versus earlier.

The Words We Use: Self-Talk Negatives and Positives

- ◆ "I am such a load," vs. "My weight doesn't define me."
- ◆ "I can't believe what a zitface I am," vs. "I'm probably the only one who notices, and it's not like I'm the only person to ever have pimples."

- "I'll die if he doesn't ask me out," vs. "He may want to go to the movies with me, but the world won't end if he says no."
- "Even if I make the team, I'll probably just ride the bench," vs. "Maybe this isn't my sport. I have the build that might be better used elsewhere."
- "I work harder than everyone else, but they get all the breaks," vs. "I wonder if there is anything else I could do to make my work stand out and be noticed?"
- "Life sucks," vs. "I'm in a rut. I'm going to shake things up!"
- "I'll never finish this degree," vs. "If I complete one chapter each day, I'll finish this course by the end of the month."

Lessons Learned: Language and Self-Talk

- The language children learn by listening to us when they are very young is the language they will use to speak to and about themselves as they develop inner speech. This development starts at a very early age, so we shouldn't wait "until they can understand what I'm talking about."
- Positive self-talk has the power to insulate kids from a lot of the slings and arrows the world aims at them. If we start young, our children can develop a dialogue of positive language that helps them filter out negative things others may say about them, helps them solve problems, and helps them turn negative situations into positive ones.
- By reducing negative self-talk, we help reduce stress and increase self-image and self-efficacy, all of which have the ability to make drug and alcohol use look less attractive as a coping mechanism.

Establish a Pattern: Give Your Children the Words They Need

Keep in Mind: In addition to instilling positive proactive language into your children's inner dialogues, you can teach them how to solve problems by giving them the actual words, sentences, and phrases that will help them handle situations with proactive positive vocabulary. This gives you and your children a chance to work out situations and role play different scenarios, which can help them to

36

not only understand human behavior but also how to react and respond in tough situations.

The Words We Use: "I can't believe you still like princesses/Legos—they're for babies!"

Every child who loves the Disney Princesses or Lego Star Wars eventually hears this from another kid at school: "Those are for babies!" This crushing blow from their friends gives the princess/Lego-loving children a choice—they can confidently defend their choice, or they can lose something that gives them great joy. Children have a whole lifetime ahead of them, most of which will be spent as adults. There is no earthly reason why childhood has to end any sooner than your children are ready for it to; but being called a baby strikes at the heart of most kids, and they will often change in ways that cause them great distress in order to avoid that label—unless you give them the words and the confidence to stand up for what they love.

Establish a Pattern: "Well, I like it!"

At our house, we started rehearsing a very simple phrase when our daughter was very young: "Well, I like it!" Shortly after beginning kindergarten, our daughter told us she no longer wanted to use her *Finding Nemo* lunchbox. When we asked her why, she just said, "I don't like it anymore." Since Nemo had always been one of her favorites, we were curious about the change of heart. After a few minutes of discussion, she told us the real reason she didn't want that particular lunchbox anymore—some of her classmates had told her that Nemo was for babies.

It's tempting in situations like this to just let it slide. We're all too busy to worry about what characters grace the front of our children's lunchboxes, but this issue is much bigger than it first appears. What's at stake here is our children's ability to self-advocate, and to stand up for what they have chosen for themselves. The children who back down and acquiesce to the wishes of the taunting element in kindergarten are often, in our experience, the same children who drink and get high in high school, even if they have absolutely no desire to, simply because they have never developed the ability to say what it is they want or don't want and to stand up for their right to choose.

In this case, and every subsequent case thereafter, we asked our daughter a very simple question: "Do you still like it?" Her response, of course, was, "Yes." We explained to her that she had every right to like whoever and whatever she wanted to, and for no other reason than it was important to her. If the other kids in her class wanted to like something else, that was fine for them, but it had no bearing on her choices.

In order for her to be able to get past the challenge that what she liked was "for babies" though, we taught her the words to say whenever anyone wanted to give her grief about a choice she made: "Well, I like it!" The beauty of this response lies in its simplicity. There is no effort made to convince the people teasing her that they are wrong, nor is there any attempt to disparage the choices the other children have made in lunch box decoration—that's not the lesson we wanted to teach. "Well, I like it," says so many things in so few words: this is what I like; you are free to like what you want; I am not a slave to what you think; you can change your mind and join me any time you want.

As she started to employ her response, the other kids stopped their comments entirely. Now, on the occasions when someone tries to tease her about a choice she has made, she has the tools and the skills to resolve the issue by standing up for herself in a positive, non-confrontational way with four little words: "Well, I like it!" (PS—It also helped when Kelly started to carry a Nemo lunchbox when she went off to teach. You might say that it is a small sacrifice to make—carrying a kids' lunchbox to work to prove a point—and that might be true, if Kelly didn't like her Nemo lunchbox so much!)

Now that our daughter is a little older, we've added a second part to the response. After she defends her choice with, "Well, I like it," she can completely take the negative out of the situation by following that with, "What do you like?" If the other child or children answer, she can very easily validate their choice (and by doing so, validate her own) with, "Oh, I like that, too."

There is so much to be said for not rising to the bait, for not making it about right and wrong, but instead making it about everyone's right to choose what they want. Maybe both children actually like the same things, but just made different choices about how to express their passions on that particular day. It sounds like such a little thing, but these are the issues that play out in much bigger ways if we don't learn how to deal with them when we are young. How your children deal with social pressure plays a huge role in whether they later choose to use drugs and alcohol when situations suggest that they do so.

Lessons Learned: Provide the Words Your Children Need

◆ We have the power to give our children the words they need to deal with situations that always crop up sooner or later. If we train them how to stand up for themselves when the stakes seem small, we give them the skills to negotiate much trickier situations that will come up when they are older.
◆ Little kids don't know that they have the right to like anything they want to, no matter what anyone else says. It's our job to teach them to believe in what they are passionate about.

Links: See links section 2B

Using the Checklist: Self-Talk

☐ What is the tone of my inner speech? Am I mostly positive, or mostly negative?

☐ Am I recognizing and eliminating my own negative self-talk?

☐ Am I helping my children build positive "I am's"?

☐ Do I need some positive "I am's" of my own?

☐ Am I sensitive to the media images my child is exposed to?

☐ Does part of my negative self-talk include thoughts that positive proactive speech is just a bunch of hooey?

☐ Am I giving my children specific words to use in situations that cause them discomfort or distress?

☐ Am I helping my children eliminate negative self-talk?

☐ Is there any chance that I secretly agree with the kids doing the teasing? Am I letting my children be who they are, or do I want them to be what I think they should be?

2.10 They Can Hear You

Keep in Mind: In her book *Raising Preschoolers*, Dr. Sylvia Rimm coined the term "Referential Speaking" to indicate the times when adults talk about children's behavior or characteristics aloud while the children can hear them. In *The Happiest Toddler on the Block*, Dr. Harvey Karp uses the term "Gossiping" to describe speech parents intend their children to hear which is meant to influence their behavior in a specific way. By using referential speaking and gossiping, you can positively influence your children as you note things about them that make you proud or impress you. This is more powerful than many parents think—one of the main reasons teens cite for not using drugs and alcohol is that they don't want to disappoint their parents. Your opinion of them really is important.

Beware: The reverse is just as powerful. If your children overhear you saying things about them that are negative, they will take it to heart in a way that will be very hard to undo. Offhand comments, or even seemingly innocuous nicknames, have the power to change your children's views of themselves. Be very careful.

The Words We Use: Expectations, Labels and Teasing

"I would be so disappointed if Bobby lied to us and went to that party."

"I am so proud of Hanna for continuing to try to get her leg up in that cartwheel."

These comments, when overheard by the children they refer to, inform their targets about some very powerful information. Bobby is on notice that he has the capacity to affect his parents through his choices. Hanna knows that her parents are aware of her hard work, and that they are proud of her.

"She's really nice, but she isn't very smart."

"He gets into everything! He's a devil."

"That girl is out of control. I don't know how were going to keep her out of trouble."

"You don't have a bit of sense! Come on! Think!"

On the other hand, these parents seem oblivious to the fact that there is a very good chance these labels will stick with their children for a long time, maybe for life. A very smart and loving friend of ours doesn't seem to appreciate how damaging it is when she says, "My kids are always going to be fat," in the presence of those very children. When you hang labels on your children, they internalize those words and very often become what you have described them to be.

"Thunder thighs." "Dumbo." "Ginger." "Carrot-top." "Dumb blonde." "Shorty."

Have you ever heard these nicknames? Did the person using them say them with a smile on their face? Did that smile, even for a second, lead you to believe that these names don't have the power to hurt? We may not realize that the nickname we use so blithely has been loathed by its owner since the first time they heard it used to refer to them. This is not intended as a condemnation of nicknames. A nickname is usually an indication of a high level of emotional connection, a special bond that the user and owner have between them. Hurtful nicknames, though, have the power to sting like bees. Just try to make sure your nickname isn't perceived by its owner as a negative label.

"Hey, is that peach fuzz I see on your lip?"

"I haven't seen that much makeup since the KISS reunion!"

Parents who say things like this probably think their comments are hilarious. Their children, on the other hand, are probably less thrilled. Very few parents actually tease their children with the intention of making them feel bad, and yet many times that is exactly what happens, especially if the children are too young to understand that you don't really mean what you are saying. It is an

42

especially egregious crime to tease a teenager about any physical aspect associated with puberty.

Lessons Learned: Expectations, Labels, Nicknames

- Children will usually try to live up to our expectations of them, be they positive or negative.
- Labels have more staying power than we think, and teasing is often interpreted by children as the truth delivered in a different way.
- Nicknames can put us on very thin ice.

Links: See links section 2C

Using the Checklist: They Can Hear You

☐ Am I using referential speech and gossiping to give my children positive insights into how I see them?

☐ Am I careful to not be overheard when discussing something negative about my child that concerns me?

☐ Have I inadvertently labeled my children in a negative way?

☐ Is there any way nicknames that refer to my children might be hurting them?

☐ Am I careful to keep teasing at an absolute minimum, and eliminate it entirely if it has the power to hurt my children's feelings?

☐ Am I watching how I speak in front of my children?

2.11 Let's Work Together

Establish a Pattern: Create a United Front

Keep in Mind: Mixed messages never fail to confuse kids, no matter what their ages. One of the most powerful weapons parents have in their arsenal is the united front. If parents can find a way to stay on the same page when they communicate with their children, they can double the power of their message. If they disagree about what is to be said and insist on sticking to their viewpoints no matter what the cost, they run the risk of confusing their kids in a big way. When parents disagree about big issues, they also force their children to choose which parent to support. In many cases, a *laissez faire* attitude on the part of one parent about certain rules of behavior will inevitably draw the children toward that parent's view and away from the other, thus creating a distinct rift children can exploit if they see an advantage in doing so.

Obviously, you and your partner don't need to be clones. Variations in outlooks and opinions keep things interesting and dynamic. Which TV show is your favorite and whether you root for the Angels or the Dodgers is not the point. The united front comes into play when you are discussing issues of health, safety, and family rules. As an example, if each parent has a different opinion about teenage alcohol use, there is going to be trouble. If mom is insistent that the children not drink until they are 21, but dad thinks that drinking is a rite of passage that all kids will eventually go through, which parent do you think the average teen is going to migrate toward?

It's not really reasonable to assume that you will agree about all these issues as they arise. It pays to discuss them beforehand, in case you each need to amend your opinions so you can meet somewhere in the middle. Remember that you do not need to agree on all things, but you do need to agree what you will present to your children about the position you have taken as a team. When you present a united front, you provide your children with a sense of continuity and comfort—a feeling of predictability and safety.

One of the biggest challenges parents face when trying to present a united front occurs in the case of divorce, especially if the process was or is contentious. If parents have to speak to each other only through counsel, it will be almost impossible to create a nuanced, unified message that will be presented to their children as a family value. We've all been witness to, on some level, the struggles parents face when one or both of them try to curry the favor of the children by playing the part of the fun parent. On the other hand, the one who tries to be the disciplinarian will almost automatically be seen as the shrew or the harpy; the taskmaster or the jerk.

We routinely witness the difficulties divorce causes for all members of the family. One of the first casualties is often communication. All each parent is left with is their own personal sense of what is best for the children. We would urge any parents caught up in this to make their best efforts to put aside their animosities as best they can, but to stay true to what they think is best for their children no matter what the short term downsides might be. Children we work with regularly chafe against the rules their parents lay out for them, and yet in their private moments they admit that if their parents didn't do that, they would feel less safe and less loved.

Even if you end up being the lone voice that speaks about rules and values and character, be that voice to the best of your ability. Tell your children that family values travel with them wherever they go. We are not in any way trying to encourage you to instruct your children to ignore the other parent, but be as clear as you can about how you feel about the subject and why it is important to you. Use "I" statements. Keep using your language patterns we discussed earlier. Take every opportunity to involve extended family members and supportive friends in your conversations about family values. Parenting is a long-run proposition, and people who make the choice to truly parent will eventually come to be seen as the ones who actually cared, even if they have to wait until their children have children of their own before they come to that realization. It boils down to being able to look in the mirror and maintain a level of self-talk that is positive and comforting, as opposed to negative and filled with guilt.

Lessons Learned: Unified Front

♦ A unified front provides children with a comforting continuity, no matter what they say at the time that unified message is being communicated to them.

♦ Mixed messages create an atmosphere of confusion.

♦ Uniformity of message is not the default setting—you should make a point of discussing your respective positions on the big issues, like drugs and alcohol.

Using the Checklist: Let's Work Together

☐ Are the adults in our family striving to present a unified front when discussing issues of health, safety, and family values?

2.12 The Drug Talk

Keep in Mind: It's not what you say that can cause you the most trouble; it's what you don't say. Most parents wait way to long to start talking about drugs with their children. As we said earlier, young children are fully capable of understanding information about drugs, as long as it is delivered in an age-appropriate manner. Also, drug lectures are just like all other parental lectures—one of the least effective methods of communicating with your children.

We must constantly be on the lookout for teachable moments, and take those small openings as opportunities to talk about drugs and alcohol in the context they are presented. If you wait too long to start the conversation, your children may run the risk of getting their drug education from a variety of unreliable sources—their peers; older siblings or students at school; movies and TV; and advertising. Once your children process this misinformation as fact, you'll struggle mightily to get it straightened out.

The Words We Don't Use: Concerns that Prevent Parents from Talking About Drugs and Alcohol

◆ A lot of parents we meet believe that their kids never think about drugs and alcohol, and that talking about these things will only serve to awaken their curiosity.

◆ Some parents worry that they might make drugs sound attractive.

◆ Many parents feel they know so little about the subject that they are worried about giving the wrong information, or that they will come off as totally unintelligent.

◆ There is a pervasive terror parents have—if they try to talk to their children about drugs, the kids will turn the tables on them and ask about the parents' drug and alcohol history.

The issues listed here are common, but that doesn't mean they justify avoiding discussions about drugs and alcohol. Children tend to be curious long before their parents imagine—Kelly was amazed a few years ago to see a number of first grade students miming the act of smoking cigarettes in their classroom. That same year, we both saw drawings done in that classroom of wine bottles and wine glasses. Later, we both wondered whether their parents were aware of this behavior, and what they would think if they had witnessed it.

The act of talking about substances does not in and of itself make them attractive. It's much more likely that images of their use in movies and on TV, or inappropriate behaviors on the part of the parents are the source of children's attraction to drug and alcohol use. If we start to talk honestly and age-appropriately to our young children about the effects of drugs and alcohol on human health, we can get ahead of the issue in a proactive way; but remember that it's not really how much you know about drugs that has the most powerful effect here—it's the fact that you have created a warm, open, non-judgmental environment that invites discussion. Children who feel listened to and supported when they discuss difficult topics are very likely to continue those discussions as they get older.

Children asking questions about parents' past use of drugs and alcohol is a complex issue, and we discuss it extensively in *Not All Kids Do Drugs*. For most of the parents reading this handbook, your children are too young for you to worry about what to say when they ask you if you ever did drugs. If a little kid asks you about your past use, you simply don't answer the question—change the direction of the discussion. What you choose to tell your children about your past as they get older is a very personal choice, but we recommend you do some research before they reach middle and high school.

Establish a Pattern: Be Proactive

◆ We'll say it again: Take a few moments each day to educate yourself about drugs and alcohol.
◆ Look for teachable moments that allow you to voice your opinion in an appropriate, timely way.
◆ Talk early and often. By establishing drugs and alcohol as ongoing topics of discussion, you create a sense of familiarity and eliminate the stress of the drug lecture.
◆ Speak from your heart about how you feel about your children, their health, their futures, and why you don't want drug use and alcohol abuse in their lives.
◆ Don't wait until after an incident of use to convey your thoughts and expectations.

◆ Don't minimize the dangers of drug and alcohol use or understate the difficulties involved with quitting smoking in an effort to comfort your children about your use or the use of a close relative. Misinformation leads to confusion, and confusion can lead to bad decisions.

A Different Perspective on Drug Discussions: The Other Side of the User

It is certainly possible that your children will not use drugs and alcohol in their teens. Obviously, we hope that's the case—it's the reason for writing this handbook! Even if you truly believe your children will never use anything, however, that doesn't mean they don't need to talk about the issue.

At a recent conference we attended, many parents were quick to assure us that their homeschooled children didn't need drug education—drugs were simply not a problem because their environment insulated them from exposure. Upon meeting with the children of these parents, though, we were overwhelmed by how many of them were deeply troubled by friends who were experiencing difficulties with drug and alcohol use. Most of the kids in our sessions were clearly non-users, but they desperately wanted to help their friends who were partying. While the parents we spoke to may, in most cases, have achieved their goal of protecting their own children from use by removing them from the school environment, even these incredibly controlled climates hadn't succeeded at preventing drugs from becoming an issue in their children's lives.

Unfortunately, because there was little or no ongoing discussion of drugs happening in these children's lives, they lacked even the most fundamental skills in dealing with the repercussions of the use happening in their friends' lives.

Actually, discussing drug and alcohol use by others is a great way to talk about the issue in a way that doesn't make your children feel that they are the ones being judged. Finding out how your children feel about the decisions other kids have made around drugs and alcohol can give you an eye into how they feel about their own challenges.

Generally, it's a good idea to avoid directly criticizing their friends. If a specific issue has arisen about a friend who is currently experiencing drug or alcohol problems, then by all means you should talk it over, but try to steer clear of expressing any negative comments you may have about your children's social circle. On the other hand, it's great if you can also talk about people who have chosen to not use substances. Your children's non-using friends are a marvelous opportunity to discuss the benefits of lifestyles that are free from drug and alcohol use.

Keep in Mind: Teens are regularly motivated to "save" their friends from trouble. If you have established an environment that encourages your children to discuss problems they are experiencing, you will be able to give guidance on how your children can be supportive friends while maintaining enough separation to remain safe.

Lessons Learned: Talking About Drugs

- Talking about drugs and alcohol is an ongoing discussion, not a one-time sit down lecture.
- It's often less about what you know and more about what kind of conversational climate you have created.
- Be proactive. Worry less and talk more, but try to do so in the context of teachable moments.
- When you talk to your children about drugs and alcohol, it isn't just about their use. Often, they are concerned about friends or family members who are having trouble.
- Lying will eventually catch up with you. If you don't know an answer, don't make one up. Do some research about what to say if your children ask you about your past drug and alcohol experience.

Using the Checklist: The Drug Talk

- ☐ Am I talking to my children about drugs and alcohol on a regular basis?

- ☐ Have I told my children how I feel about this subject?

- ☐ Have I found a way to incorporate the topic of the other side of the user?

- ☐ Am I being careful about the stories my children hear about drug use?

- ☐ Do I have positive role models to discuss?

2.13 Establishing Patterns of Listening

Keep in Mind: Listening is just as important as talking; maybe more so. The old maxim about having two ears and one mouth and using them in that proportion is not lost here. We've spent so much time writing about the importance of language, but what good is language if nobody knows how to listen? When we listen well, we show that we value the person and what they are saying. If we take care to understand what is being said, we are much better equipped to respond in an appropriate fashion. Steven Covey found it so important he dedicated an entire chapter to listening in *The Seven Habits of Highly Effective People*: "Seek First to Understand, Then to be Understood."

The Words We Use: "Um, yeah, I'm listening."

Actually, you probably aren't. Listening takes time, energy, and commitment, three things most of us have in very short supply. It can be especially daunting to maintain focus when your child is in the seventh minute of a story about what SpongeBob has been up to recently, the telling of which is occurring while you're trying to prepare dinner and answer emails. What you're doing is certainly important, you're probably dead tired, and you may have a thousand other things on your mind, but if your children have taken the time to talk to you, what they are talking about is probably pretty important to them. They may think they are doing you the world's biggest favor when they share with you the hilarity of what happened at recess that day. Unfortunately, if you don't make a supreme effort to listen when it seems not to be important, your children will stop coming to you by the time it really is. It wasn't used in exactly the same context, but something one of Jonathan's drug counselors once said applies equally well here: "It's amazing how quickly someone will stop throwing you the ball if you make absolutely no effort whatsoever to catch it."

Establish a Pattern: Check for Understanding

"I'm not sure I understand. Who got blown up?"

If you don't understand what your children are talking about, don't worry, you're not losing your mind. Sometimes it can take a few tries to understand, but consider this good practice for later, when the plotlines of your teens' social lives will rival the most intricately woven soap opera. Learning how to check for understanding now will pay big dividends later, because it establishes a communication style that shows you value what your children are talking about. Try to summarize what they are telling you; if you didn't quite get the point, try again. Frustrating? Yes. Worth it? Absolutely.

Establish a Pattern: How Do You Listen?

Think about how you listen to people (not just your kids).

◆ When people talk to you, are you listening, or are you thinking about something else?
◆ Do you find yourself nodding your head in agreement when you actually couldn't say what the person speaking is talking about if your life depended on it? If so, you're guilty of pretending to listen.
◆ Do you find yourself spacing out—actually coming out of a fog to the realization you have no idea how long it's been since you heard a word the speaker has said?
◆ Are you formulating your response in your head while the other person is still speaking?
◆ Do you find yourself finishing other people's sentences for them, since you already know what they are going to say?
◆ Are you letting past experiences with the speaker prejudice what you're hearing and interpreting?

These examples are just a few of the ways to tell if you have lost the ability to listen, or possibly that you never learned to listen in the first place. Becoming aware of how we do something allows us to change the way we do it in the future. If you were to ask people if they are good listeners, most would probably say yes (if they heard the question in the first place, that is). In fact, listening is more and more considered to be a lost art; a forgotten skill. If we want to build strong relationships with our children, we would be well served to do as Lily Tomlin once observed, and "listen with an intensity most people save for talking."

Establish a New Pattern: Changing How We Listen

♦ When listening, just listen. After the speaker is done, take a moment to reflect on what was said, and then formulate your response based upon the entirety of what was said, not just the first few words or sentences.
♦ If you need to, jot down a key word or two during long statements so you don't have to devote a part of your awareness to holding an important point in your head the whole time.
♦ Repeat back what it is you think was said. If you missed the point, have the speaker restate their thoughts in another way so you might better understand.
♦ Ask open-ended questions when speaking with your children. "How was the game?" might get you a mumbled reply of, "OK." A better response will probably result from the question, "What was the best part of the game for you?"
♦ Try to remember, if someone has chosen to speak to you, what they are speaking about is probably important to them. Try to show them that they are important to you by listening to them.

Lessons Learned: Listening

Everyone wants to be heard. By listening to your children, you send the message that you care what is going on in their lives. If you listen to their dramas when they are eight, they are more likely to keep you informed about the dramas they experience at 15. If you want to communicate effectively with someone, you have to hear his or her side of the story. Remember, your goal is to keep the conversations with your children about drugs and alcohol in the forefront for their entire young lives. One of the best ways to accomplish that goal is to be an effective listener.

Using the Checklist: Listening

☐ What kind of listener am I?

☐ How might I best improve my listening skills?

☐ Am I practicing reflective listening?

☐ Am I listening to what my kids have to say?

☐ Am I encouraging my kids to talk, or am I cutting them off when I become frustrated?

☐ Am I trying to seek first to understand, and then to be understood?

Applying Positive Proactive Language in Daily Life

2.14 Talking About Money

Keep in Mind: Money problems are a major source of stress. Money issues are commonly cited as the number one cause of stress in marriages. When we start talking to our children about money management at an early age, we are proactively teaching skills that can change their lives. Most people, no matter how much money they have, find they don't have enough if they aren't actively trying to live within a budget. One of Jonathan's bosses used to say, "Remember, the average person operates at a level that is equal to 110% of their income." Talk about stress! Money woes are associated with poor self image as well. You can save your children a lot of trouble if you help them learn the language of fiscal responsibility.

When our daughter wants something, we make sure to include her in the process of being able to afford it. At the age of five, when she first expressed a desire to get an American Girl doll, we set up a program where she could earn money by doing extra jobs around the house, over and above what she is expected to contribute as a member of the family. If she got monetary gifts for birthdays or holidays, she was allowed to use half of each amount toward her goal, and the other half went into her savings account. When the big day arrived, we went to the American Girl store at the Grove in Los Angeles and rode the escalator up to where the big displays are, and that's when the most magical thing happened.

We were greeted by a young woman who started to talk to us about what we were looking for. When our daughter told her which doll she wanted and how long she had been working and saving her money, the young woman told her how great she thought is was to be willing to put in so much effort. We parted ways, and went off to find our Julie doll. As we were getting ready to check out, the young woman returned and gave our daughter a huge shopping bag full of clothes and accessories specifically chosen for our daughter's doll. As she handed the gift to our astonished little girl, she said, "We appreciate how hard you've worked to save up for your doll. That's something we think is very valuable in a little girl. You should be very proud of yourself." It was one of those rare moments when all the effort you put into teaching your child a valuable life lesson pays off in a measurable, concrete way. What a wonderful thing that young woman did to reinforce what we had been working on; and what a great object lesson for our daughter.

When you can, engage your children in money matters as soon as possible. When you're at the supermarket, give them a calculator they can use to keep track of how much you are spending. Even if you don't really need to, set a limit on how much you can spend that day. Occasionally, you can purposefully exceed your budget, and then work with your children on what to put back in order to get under your spending limit. By doing so, you can teach them a sense of perspective when it comes to money. A headmaster at one of our schools once said, "One of the worst crimes you can commit against a child is to give them everything they want." Great deprivation is damaging to children, but so is limitless reward for no effort.

Using the Checklist: Talking About Money

☐ Am I letting my kids add up purchases on the calculator?

☐ Am I talking about how much managing a household costs?

☐ Am I talking about how to save, earn, and budget?

☐ Am I conscious of the "Costco Effect," and actively trying to avoid impulse buying?

☐ Am I talking to my children about the consequences of poor money management?

2.15 Talking About Movies

Keep in Mind: We know quite a few parents who don't let their children watch TV and severely restrict the movies they are allowed to see. While their goals may be admirable, in that they want to protect their children from the increasing presence of violence, profanity, sex and irresponsibility portrayed in the media lately, we think they are also missing out on a goldmine of teachable moments. As we observed earlier, children as young as three or four can see Cruella De Vil smoking without suffering permanent damage, and the parents can have a field day discussing with their children all the harmful aspects of smoking. They can point to the teeth, the lungs, and the heart to illustrate the parts of the body which can be damaged by cigarette use.

As children grow older, parents can continue to point out smoking scenes and, with their children's participation, analyze those scenes with an eye toward how cigarette use is portrayed in the movies and whether that portrayal matches up with reality. When we raise children who are media-literate, we equip them with the skills to analyze marketing messages and the resiliency to resist falling prey to images designed to make them feel inferior or un-cool if they don't look or act a certain way. Certainly one of the most insidious challenges young people face today is overcoming the messages about body shape constantly blaring at them from all sides, and yet how are they to develop the skills they need without practice and guidance? Movies create teachable moments, if we use them correctly.

As with everything else we have covered so far, though, this requires effort on the part of the parents. It would be highly inadvisable to wade blindly into a movie you've never seen before with your four year old sitting at your side. You'll never be able to react fast enough to shield your children's eyes and ears from a scene that is inappropriate if all of you are watching the movie for the first time, and that means you have to preview the movie before you allow your children to see it. You can do this on your own, if you never intend to sleep again, or you can follow certain rating organizations' suggestions as to the appropriateness of a film or TV show. We frequently check a site called Common Sense Media at *www.commonsensemedia.org/* for guidance about the content of any movie we might plan to see with our daughter.

The Words We Use: "Loopy."

In our Myths Around the World classes, kids in 4th and 5th grade often have a hard time understanding what getting drunk means. Terms like disinhibition, discoordination, and delirium haven't got a chance of getting a meaningful message across. Children do, however, seem to immediately understand what we mean when we say the word "loopy." As we mentioned in the opening section of this handbook, we have used a scene from the movie *Ratatouille* as a teachable moment to talk about intoxication in a way our daughter can understand at the age of seven or eight. When the character Linguini gets drunk with the evil chef Skinner, he starts to slur his words and talk in a very nonsensical way. When we described him as acting loopy, she quickly grasped what we meant. This is the same as the opportunity provided by the smoking scene discussed earlier, in that it provides an opening to discuss how alcohol changes the way people feel, has the power to make them act in ways they usually wouldn't when sober, and can cause them to fall and hurt themselves by making them clumsy.

Again, as your children enter middle and high school, you can delve more deeply into the issues of alcoholism, cirrhosis of the liver, cancer, DUI, etc.; and discuss whether scenes in movies that depict heavy, ongoing alcohol abuse do so in realistic or misleading ways.

Establish a Pattern: Pause and Talk

Whenever you are watching TV or a movie with your children, use your remote control to pause the action when necessary. Discuss with your children what is being shown, with an eye toward how realistic the scene is. Obviously, if you go too far with this, your children will never want to watch anything with you again; but if you start young, it will become your pattern of behavior.

Try to compare what is happening on screen with what happens in real life. Questions like, "Do you think that's what would happen if you or I were to do that?" and, "Is that really the way things usually work out?" can help you talk with your children about actions and their consequences.

Yes, we're aware of the concept of suspension of disbelief and the joy one can get from becoming immersed in the story—we would never pause the film to discuss whether Harry Potter's wand is real or not—but if outrageous scenes in movies are perceived by your children as real, their understanding of drug and alcohol issues will be wildly inaccurate.

Lessons Learned: Media and Teachable Moments

Various media provide a rich variety of teachable moments. Used cautiously and wisely, they are wonderful tools that open up opportunities for you to have meaningful conversations with your children about a limitless variety of topics, including drugs and alcohol.

Using the Checklist: Talking About Movies

☐ Am I using movies and other media to start conversations with my children?

☐ Am I using overly technical language before my children understand the basic concepts?

2.16 Medicine Cabinets; OTC Drugs

Keep in Mind: Prescription medications and over-the-counter (OTC) medicines (such as headache relievers, muscle ache and fever reducers, and cough medicines) are still drugs! These should be included in any conversations you have about drugs and alcohol, as they have the potential to be misused and can cause great harm. We have to dispel the idea that if one is good, then three will be three times as effective.

Some OTC medications, such as acetaminophen products like Tylenol, have an effective dose that is extremely close to their dangerous dose, and great care must be exercised in order to avoid injury or death. Conversations about these types of drugs should continue well past elementary school—we constantly encounter high school and college students who have no idea that OTC medications can be dangerous.

Cause for Concern: Prescription and OTC Drug Abuse Are at an All-time High

Prescription drug abuse has reached epidemic proportions. In 2010, 10% of high school seniors abused hydrocodone (Vicodin), an opiate pain pill, and almost 5% abused oxycodone (OxyContin), a timed-release opiate responsible for numerous overdose deaths each year. In 2009, prescription drug overdoses eclipsed automobile accidents as a cause of death! About twice as many young people are receiving prescription medications from their doctors today than were a decade ago. That doesn't mean these young people are receiving these medications illegally or inappropriately, but it does mean there is a much larger supply of prescription medications that can be diverted to people willing to abuse or misuse them. This is a huge concern, because teenagers as a group are operating under the impression that OTC and prescription medications are safer because they come from a doctor, a pharmacist, or a drug store.

Unfortunately, society hasn't kept pace with the risk posed by these medications. Far too many homes still have abusable medicines stored in completely unsupervised locations, the most typical being the medicine chest. Maybe we should start calling the medicine chest the "potential to kill my children drug overdose, addiction, and death locker" instead, and see if attitudes about the compounds kept there change. The alarming statistic most parents don't seem to be aware of is that the overwhelming majority of medications children abuse are obtained from friends, relatives, and family members either for free or by taking them without permission. Any medication with the potential for abuse should be in a locked, monitored location in the home. It is time for parents to wake up to the dangers these drugs pose and take actions to limit their availability to the times when they are being actively dispensed for legitimate reasons.

While many of these prescription and OTC drugs are abused at parties and social events, a sizable number of them are used by teens to increase their capacity to accomplish a task, as in the case of teenagers taking ADHD medications, which are typically stimulants, to increase the amount of time they can study without getting sleepy. In many cases, the danger is enhanced by the failure to consider how an abused medication may be interfering with other medicines the person might be taking legally and appropriately for legitimate medical needs.

The Words We Use: Medicine is Not "Candy."

◆ Be sure your children know that medicines are drugs, and are safe only when taken as directed.
◆ Be very clear: medicine is NEVER candy! Do not say, "It's yummy," or, "Look, mommy will take a teaspoon first— Mmmmm, that's delicious!" This teaches that sharing medicine is OK and that it should be enjoyed because it tastes good.

Establish a Pattern: Medicine and OTC Drugs

◆ Talk to your children about the fact that medicines are drugs, and that we don't need to be afraid of them, but we do need to respect their powers to help and to harm.
◆ Make it a rule: Your children are not allowed to take any medicine, no matter what kind, unless you know about it and have given permission for it to be used.
◆ Teach your children to check for expiration dates. This includes commonly used medications like Tylenol, Advil and Aleve, etc.

If you take expired medicine, it might not work as well as it should, which could lead to more frequent or larger doses than are safe. Some medicines, such as tetracycline, become toxic after the expiration date.

- Teach your children the importance of following the directions that come with medications. As a first step: You know that folded piece of paper you pull out of the box and immediately chuck into the garbage? Stop doing that! There is a wealth of information about dosage and safe use on it that you should take the time to read. At a minimum, you should read all sections that have anything to do with dose, safety, warnings, dangers, and especially a section called "contraindications," which warns you about other drugs, foods, and beverages that should not be taken at the same time the medicine is used.

- If your children are too young to read, at least let them see and hear you read the directions aloud. Teach them to follow directions for medicine to the letter.

- We know it's really hard to stand by and watch your children suffer when they are sick or in pain, but for young children, sometimes the medicine is worse than the symptoms. In the past few years, the FDA has issued numerous warnings directing parents to stop using cold medications for children under the age of two. Thousands of emergency room visits and dozens of deaths have been reported as a result of reactions to these medications.

- In 2011, new FDA warnings also cautioned against the use of solutions or gels which contain benzocaine on children under two, due to the risk of a rare but possibly fatal condition that limits the amount of oxygen their red blood cells can carry. The most commonly used medicines of this type are drops used to reduce the pain associated with teething in infants.

- Talk to your children about the dangers of sharing medications, either by taking medicine intended for others or by giving medicine intended for them to other children.

- Reading labels doesn't stop at medicines. Help your children to read and understand other labels as well. Energy drinks are currently not required to list the amount of caffeine they contain, although some do in an effort to draw in people looking for a big jolt of caffeine.

◆ Labels on foods list ingredients by their predominance, with the highest percentages first, so if sugar, high fructose corn syrup or other sugary ingredients are high up on the list, you can be pretty sure it's not health food. Kelly also adds in her classes on reading labels, "If you can't pronounce it, you should think twice about putting it in your mouth."

What to do When Medicine Tastes Disgusting

◆ If you have difficulty getting your children to take medicine because the taste is disgusting, have a special cup with ginger ale, juice, sparkling water with fruit, etc., so they can immediately rinse the taste out of their mouths after they take the specified dose. Unless you want to be washing cups all day long, you might want to use paper cups in this case so you don't have a bunch of germy glasses floating around your house. You can help your children decorate the cups in such a way that they look forward to using them.
◆ Another successful way to encourage children to take distasteful medicine is to create a graph or chart they can mark on or put stickers on to track their timing and dosage of medicine.
◆ Some kids love to let out a big "YUK!" or "UGH!" right after they take their dose. You can help by joining in—include a really ugly face if you want to make them laugh.
◆ Get a dinger or teacher bell (the kind with the little plunger you push down on to make the bell ring) they can use to celebrate their accomplishment.

Lessons Learned: Medicine Cabinets, OTC Drugs

◆ Medicines, be they prescription or OTC, are still drugs.
◆ Prescription drug abuse has reached epidemic proportions.
◆ Medicine is not candy.
◆ Teach your kids to read and follow labels to the letter.

Links: See links section 2D

Using the Checklist: Medicine Cabinets, OTC Drugs

☐ Have I checked my "potential to kill my children drug overdose, addiction, and death locker" for expired drugs and drugs with the potential for abuse?

☐ Have I put abusable, dangerous, and addictive drugs in my home in a secure, monitored location?

☐ Am I being specific about the way I discuss medicine around my children?

☐ Am I reading my labels?

☐ Am I teaching my children about labels, dose information and warnings?

☐ Am I treating drugs the way they would be treated at a pharmacy?

☐ Do I have a system to give distasteful medicine to my kids?

Self-Medicating vs. Scientific Studies

The Internet is awash in comments by young people who talk about how smoking marijuana makes their ADHD or ADD symptoms lessen in intensity or disappear completely. A study from 2009 showed that about one third of teenagers who smoked marijuana did so for medical reasons as opposed to using it to get high.

On a different note, various studies done over the years at the Universities of California Irvine and San Diego with patients suffering from Multiple Sclerosis have found that smoking marijuana measurably reduced perceived levels of both pain and muscle spasticity. In some of these studies, MS patients reported pain and spasticity relief even as their conditions worsened—in other words, they felt better as they got worse. We don't doubt for a second that the relief these young ADHD sufferers and MS patients feel is real, but children have a lot of difficulty understanding the difference between symptom relief and medical treatment. Anyone suffering from a condition or illness welcomes symptom relief, but the question then becomes, "At what cost?"

The MS patients in one of the UCSD studies definitely had lower levels of pain and spasticity, but they also suffered measurable cognitive deficits as a result of smoking marijuana. We know this because the researchers kept detailed track of the effects smoking marijuana had on the patients.

The young people with ADHD and ADD, however, are rarely taking part in scientific medical studies when they smoke marijuana. They have simply discovered, typically by accident or by listening to the stories of others like them, that smoking marijuana makes them feel better. They have no idea, however, if other effects are taking place that they can't measure, because they are looking at it from the perspective of someone who is trying to assess their own current mental state while under the influence of a drug.

A person can't perceive something accurately if their perceptions are altered by a drug, and that's the big problem for people who end up self-medicating—they have no idea what the drug they are taking to make themselves feel better is actually costing them. All medications have consequences associated with their use, both good and bad; and we decide whether to continue or discontinue their use by balancing the pros and the cons that result from taking them. When children self-medicate by smoking marijuana, these positives and negatives are very unclear or, many times, unidentified. Self-medication is often a maze of unknowns, with symptom relief as its only reward.

2.17 Talking About Self-Medicating

Keep in Mind: Some children discover, quite accidentally, that a compound, beverage or food they are ingesting makes them feel better in a perceivable way.

The Words We Use: Explaining Self-Medication

Lots of parents would be very reluctant to discuss marijuana smoking and ADHD symptom relief with their fourth graders, and that's probably appropriate. Unfortunately, Internet chat boards are populated by many people who describe smoking marijuana and experiencing such symptom relief at ages as young as 12. So, what are we to do? The best path seems to be the one we have already followed so many times in this section—start talking to our children early about the concepts associated with consuming anything that changes the way we act or feel, and how doing so can carry repercussions well beyond our ability to see them clearly.

One way to do this would be to refer to the dosage instructions on medications. Almost all OTC medicines have, as a part of their warnings, a caution against taking them for longer than a specified period of time. Almost everyone, even the most dedicated of instruction dodgers, has heard or read the words, "If your condition worsens, or if symptoms persist for more than seven days, discontinue use and consult your doctor." The reason for this statement is that continued, long-term use of the medication might be masking a more serious condition that, if left untreated, could result in considerable repercussions. If we talk to our children about not using medications to mask symptoms when they are young, they will be well versed in the concept when we talk to them about using other substances for similar reasons when they get older. This really matters—we have yet to see a bag of marijuana that has the label, "If your condition worsens....."

Self-Medicating and Self-Awareness: Caffeine

The discussion gets a little cloudier when we broach the subject of caffeine. An overwhelming percentage of American adults use caffeine—80% consume it regularly, and 20% consume a daily dose that is associated with potential addiction (>350mg). Unfortunately, a lot of young people regularly consume large doses of caffeine either through coffee, soft drinks, or energy drinks. This is where the "Do as I say, not as I do" issue can crop up for a lot of parents, but there is distinct difference between adults and children when it comes to substances like alcohol and caffeine. Adults, because their central nervous systems are mature and well established, run a much lower risk of detrimental effects from moderate, occasional use of caffeine and alcohol than kids and teenagers do. When talking about the use of caffeine with your children, remember that this isn't a case of right and wrong, it's a case of healthy and safe versus unhealthy and unsafe.

What kinds of situations might cause young people to abuse caffeine or use it to self-medicate? A few are:

◆ To study for longer periods without the associated loss of focus or increased fatigue.
◆ To be able to focus, if they suffer from undiagnosed ADD or ADHD.
◆ To increase athletic performance.
◆ To engage socially, both because of the stimulant nature of caffeine and the social nature of the coffee bar settings in which it is often used.

Once again, you've probably noticed that the drug, in this case caffeine, isn't the problem. Instead, it is being used in situations where there is something else missing which ultimately, because it is missing, makes the use of a drug more inviting or attractive.

Let's take a quick look at what we mean:

◆ Effective study skills include time management, taking breaks (chunking it down, covered extensively in Part 3), and adequate sleep.
◆ ADHD and ADD are medical conditions. While drugs are regularly used to treat them, so are numerous other types of interventions and therapies that require professional assessment, not another cup of coffee.

- Athletic performance derived from caffeine use is just another form of cheating. Some sports actually test for caffeine use. True athletic performance is achieved through practice, training, diet, adequate sleep, and professional input when necessary; but certainly not with caffeine.
- Social skills are learned through practice that, while sometimes painful and embarrassing, will result in abilities that last our entire adult lives. Social interactions fueled by drugs teach but one thing—"I need drugs to succeed socially."

Unfortunately, the problem of self-medicating gets more serious as the drugs get stronger. Students who constantly study while under the influence of caffeine might be tempted to up the ante by abusing ADHD medications when they get further into their academic careers. The abuse of ADHD medications as study aids on college campuses is well documented. Our discussions with our older children must also include the concepts of pill sharing and pharmaceutical misuse as well.

This problem can't be dealt with solely by talking to our children about it. Parents have to keep a close eye on their children, even when they are quite young, so they can stay alert to patterns of behavior that may indicate the presence to self-medication. Communication and observation both play a role in keeping this troubling trend in check.

Lessons Learned: Self-Medicating

Young people inadvertently or purposefully end up in situations where they are self-medicating. The risks and side effects of doing so are rarely apparent to them, so it is incumbent upon parents to talk to their children about taking any medication or substance that changes the way they feel or increases their ability to accomplish a particular task. OTC and prescription medication instruction sheets are a great place to start, and you can expand your range of substances discussed as your children get older.

Links: See links section 2E

Using the Checklist: Self-Medicating

☐ Am I being careful about self-prescribing and self-medicating?

☐ Do I have a clear picture of how much caffeine my children are consuming?

☐ Have I discussed the safe, supervised use of medications in our home?

☐ Do my children need my permission before they consume beverages that contain high levels of caffeine—energy drinks, brewed coffee, etc.?

☐ Am I closely monitoring the use of medications in my home, both pharmaceutical and OTC?

2.18 Yes and No Talk

Keep in Mind: It's perfectly OK to say no to your children, but we regularly see parents who struggle with the use of this simple word. It is also, however, perfectly OK to say yes to your children as well. The trick is in knowing how and when to use each, and how to use the word yes to open up completely new worlds of no.

The Words We Use: "No..."

"No, you can't go to the party." You are probably perfectly justified in not letting your children attend most high school parties. A good number of them are unsupervised, and the majority of drug and alcohol use by teens occurs at parties. In fact, we are writing this handbook at the same time as we are another—titled *Where's the Party?*—that discusses the dangers posed by unsupervised teen parties. Despite the fact that you have great reasons why not to let your children go to such events, you aren't going to win any popularity contests by taking that position. We don't like to say no. We all want to be liked, and we all want to find ourselves in pleasant circumstances, but parenting often requires us to stick to our guns despite wild howls of protest over the unfairness of our decisions.

Better Words: "No, but..."

We can win back a lot of ground by simply changing the no to a "No, but..." and suggesting an alternative to the request. "No, you can't go to the party, but how about if you make some plans with a few friends to do something else. I'd be happy to drive you someplace, if you want, and I promise I won't speak." You can feel free to make suggestions as to what the alternative to the party might be, but if your teens have shown patterns in the past of utter disdain for your input, you might want to save yourself the trouble—it really depends on where you currently stand on their acceptability meter.

Even Better Still: "Yes, if..."

If you start to practice when your children are really young, by the time they are asking permission to attend parties in high school you are going to be a pro at the best answer there is: "Yes, if…" If you can find a way to say yes to most of what your children want, you might just find that you are getting most of what you want, too, as long as you connect what you each desire. "Yes, you can play Wii, if you'll just help me fold this basket of laundry first. Set the timer for 30 minutes when you play, and when it goes off, you can come help me shred some lettuce for tonight's salad."

Of course, you could say the same thing this way: "No! You are not going to play Wii until after you do your job! This basket of laundry has been sitting here all day. It's not going to fold itself, you know; and by the way, I need help getting dinner ready, too. I'm not the cook, and I'm not the maid!" If that sounds familiar, you're not alone; but that's also why so many parents we talk to have such difficulty getting their children to cooperate. Why would they? The second response has nothing to do with asking for cooperation, it is a set of demands and veiled accusations. People are just not wired to respond to such replies in a positive way; rather they just build resistance and resentments.

A speaker Jonathan saw a few years ago had a great way of framing the challenge: put your children's passions on the other side of their obligations. If your children want something, they will have to do something in order to get it, but you frame it in such a way as to rarely have to tell them no.

We use this all the time with our daughter. She knows when she's doing her homework that it's perfectly OK for her to go online and visit some of her favorite websites, as long as it is done during breaks from doing schoolwork. She sets her own timer for the allotted time to be spent online, and when it goes off, she doesn't even say a word—she pauses her game and goes back to her work. If you think about it, there's no reason not to—the sooner she gets the next section done, the sooner she can take the next break. There's no arguing, no fighting, no gnashing of teeth or wailing to the winds; she does it because it gets her what she wants.

How does this benefit you later, when your children ask you if they can go to a party? Exactly the same way it did with the basket of laundry and the shredded lettuce: with the answer, "Yes, you can go to the party, if you get me the phone number of the parents who will be supervising. If everything checks out OK, it should be alright. Oh, and I can't wait to drop by and see how much fun you're

73

having! I wish I was a teenager again!" You see? It's all in how you say it. Maybe they'll do the legwork and end up going to the party, but it's just as likely they'll realize that if you call, you're going to find out that the host's parents are going to be out of town and have no idea their house will be the site of what the Newport Beach, CA, police department refers to as a "Loud and Unruly Gathering." You said yes, but it ended up being a no—and you never had to use the word.

Lessons Learned: Yes and No

You have the right to say no to anything that represents a threat to your children's safety and health, but finding a way to say yes while still getting the same result is infinitely preferable.

Using the Checklist: Yes and No Talk

☐ Am I saying no when I could have said yes?

☐ When I say no, am I offering alternative ideas?

☐ Do I find myself saying yes just to avoid being unpopular or to head off a fight?

☐ Do I say no when necessary—when issues of health and safety are on the line?

2.19 Teaching Conflict Resolution

Keep in Mind: When two or more human beings interact, there is the potential for conflict. Giving your children the skills to resolve conflict positively for both parties will save them and you a world of grief. It boils down to self-confidence, knowing what you want, understanding what the other person wants, and the willingness to employ a little diplomacy.

Establish a Pattern: Conflict Resolution for Children

There are several schools of thought on kids learning to deal with other kids. One of the ways that was popular back in the good old days was to "let 'em fight it out." It doesn't take a whole lot of insight here to see that this theory is heavily in favor of the bigger, older, or more violent party. New research shows that children left to fight it out are seriously at risk for future emotional problems.

Another method calls for the parents to step in immediately and take the situation over. The parents speak for the children, and while this might stop conflict in the short term, it does nothing to teach them how to advocate for themselves when the parents aren't around to save them. Ultimately, children will be more successful and happy if they have the skills to resolve conflicts on their own, but still have confidence that their parents will lend a hand or step in when absolutely necessary.

Honing the skills necessary for effective conflict resolution in your home will establish a pattern of working out problems that will serve your children in all their social interactions. It is, however, usually not intuitive for younger children to be resolution minded. Maybe you're familiar with this kind of exchange:

"He hit me!"
"I did not!"
"Yes, you did, you booger brain!"
"You're a booger brain, not me!"

You know, stuff that's going to cement their status as captains of the debate team.

When children are younger, conflict resolution needs to be less about who did what and more about how we can move forward from here. Of course, you should first inquire as to the presence of blood, and if no one is in immediate need of a doctor, you can start to deal with the emotions that are boiling over. The first thing to remember is that if the children are really young, their little undeveloped brains have almost no capacity to recount a story accurately. Each party will have their own version of how things played out, neither of which will be accurate. Police departments over the years have come to understand that even adult eyewitnesses are sometimes highly unreliable, so you're probably not going to get a lot of trial-worth testimony out of a couple of young children. Squabbles usually happen fast, and young kids can't process why they did what they did because they don't really understand the concepts of forethought and the consequences that follow actions.

Young children are also in a very "me first" frame of mind that means they always think the fault lies with the other party, so if you want to save yourself a lot of wasted time, move past the blame section of the negotiation as quickly as possible.

The Words We Use: Resolving a Conflict

The following are ideas you can use to give children stepping-stones that will help them resolve issues that arise due to conflict.

- Your job is to guide the conversation. You should not provide the resolution for them; rather you lead them and help them arrive at their own solution.
- Have all of the parties involved take a big, deep breath and blow it out together. Say something like, "Take in all the good air and blow out all the frustration you feel." This is something they can all do together, which essentially gets them sharing and cooperating.
- Listen, but be aware that they will continually try to say, "But, she did this..." Just hold up your hand, say, "Stop, that isn't helping us to move forward," as many times as necessary. Guide them to use "I" statements about what happened.
- Don't let the story of what happened go on for more than a minute or two. Ask them what they think should happen to work

things out. Try to keep them in the resolution mode as much as possible.

◆ When asked what will make things right, most children will explain what behavior they won't repeat, and this is the point where you are likely to get more of the real story of what actually happened. This is also where they start to work toward the apology phase.

◆ Next, they will actually find the words to apologize to each other. This can't be you forcing them to apologize; they have to feel as though they reached this resolution on their own.

Every once in a while, parents and teachers will have to deal with the rare child who is simply a bully. If you can establish a pattern over time of aggressive or violent behavior that poses an ongoing threat to other children who interact with this child, you will have to consider other solutions. Dealing with a child who appears beyond redemption is, however, so rare that we're not going to dedicate space in this volume to dealing with that circumstance. Almost every child we've ever dealt with responded to earnest efforts to engage them with an eye toward resolution.

Keep in Mind: What goes on in the home is often reflected in the classroom. Most of the time, when we find the behavior of a child to be challenging in the classroom, consultations with faculty, administration, and counselors will reveal that their behavior is largely reflective of a problem happening at home—divorce, a death in the family, an absentee parent, alcoholism, etc. It's helpful for all involved to remember that difficult behavior is often just a child with no better way to deal with the raging emotions going on inside them.

The Words We Use: Standing in Someone Else's Shoes

Children experiencing big emotional difficulties at home will often find themselves in conflict with other children or adults. In cases when another child's ire is directed at your children, it probably has nothing to do with anything they have done. The other child may not be able to verbalize what is going on with them emotionally, but is instead lashing out in some way to deal with what they are feeling.

This is a difficult concept for young children to understand, but if you're aware of a special circumstance in the other child's life, you can teach your children to empathize with the difficulties the other person is dealing with.

"Why do you think your friend is saying mean things about you?"
"I don't know! I didn't do anything to her!"
"Is she having any trouble at school?"
"The teacher has sent her to the office twice this week!"
"Did she say anything about problems at home?"
"She said her dad doesn't live with her family any more. He lives in a hotel now. She's really sad, and I saw her crying at recess the other day while we were playing."
"How do you think that feels for her, to have her dad move out?"
"Really sad."
"If you felt like that, would you still act the same way you do now?"
"Probably not."
"Please try to remember that the next time she says something mean. It probably has nothing to do with you at all. Your friend is really hurting right now, and she needs your understanding."

Of course, you won't be privy to all the secret ins and outs of other people's marital difficulties, nor should you be, but the real point here is to remember that other people are regularly struggling with challenges we have no clue about. These challenges have a huge impact on how they relate to others, and if they are acting in a way that seems purposefully hurtful or unkind, it usually has exactly nothing to do with anything we've done. When you speak to your children about conflict they are experiencing with others, it pays to keep this in mind, and to speak with them about it. Please don't think your children's teachers will be able to do this work—they are ethically bound to not speak openly with your children about difficulties other students may be experiencing at home.

2.20 Socialize Your Children

Keep in Mind: Teach your children how to interact with others. Some children are just naturally gregarious. We have a nickname for the son of a friend of ours—we call him "The Mayor." Once, when he was about eight, the family took a vacation on a cruise ship. His parents told us they just shook their heads as total strangers continued to greet their son by name, yelling to him from across the room like they were old friends. He's just a socially gifted kid. Other children aren't so gifted. When our daughter was younger, we were regularly baffled by the way other children her age responded to her. Typically, she would greet them with a smile and say, "Hi! My name is ____. What's your name?" Nine times out of ten, the response would be a completely blank stare accompanied by absolutely zero response.

We work with a lot of children every year, and we understand that there are many different levels of social comfort—a shy kid will be less likely to engage, no matter what you teach them about social conventions. But we think a lot of children would be better served if their parents would take the time to teach them how to comfortably interact with others from outside the home environment. Socially inept children will often grow up to be socially inept teens, and that unease will create a higher likelihood that these children will be the ones who use drugs and alcohol as solutions to the uncomfortable feelings they have at parties.

The Words We Use: Interacting With Other Kids

- Practice introductions: "My name is ..."
- Teach them a few common questions to ask when meeting another child for the first time: "What's your name?" "How old are you?" "What grade are you in school?" "Do you have a dog?" "Do you have brothers and sisters?" "Do you know how to ride a bike?" "What's your favorite animal?" "What's your favorite TV show?"
- Practice these questions with them. You might want to role play with some of their favorite stuffed animals. You can do the voice for the animal.

- Role play situations where your children may need to work out problems with another child. The words, "I'm sorry," have alarming power to resolve conflict. Teach your children to say them.
- Young children don't understand looking up and making eye contact when speaking, and at certain developmental points it's not even what they are supposed to do; but as your children get older, remind them to look up when they speak, and to face the person they are addressing.

Keep in Mind: Teach your children how to interact with adults. Equally as important to teaching your children to interact well with others their age is teaching them to interact well with adults. Your children's lives are going to be constantly filled with adults they are going to be forced to deal with. If your children are skilled at interacting with adults, they will gain a lot of subtle benefits from that ability. Watch an adult's face when they are greeted by a child. If the child comes off as sullen or uncommunicative, the adult will often react with a sense of displeasure that is apparent in their expression. On the other hand, when they are greeted by a child who knows how to make eye contact, shake hands, smile, and speak clearly and politely, the adult's face will often break into a surprised look of great pleasure. Why would you not want your children to have the advantage of adults who immediately like them and respond positively to them?

Teaching your children the skills involved in interacting with adults will open multiple doors and create opportunities that might not exist otherwise.

The Words We Use: Interacting With Adults

- "My name is Bobby. It's a pleasure to meet you."
- "Thank you for having me over for a play date. I had a very nice time."
- "I'm having trouble with this assignment. Will you please help me figure it out?"
- "I'm having problems with a friend of mine. May I make an appointment to meet with you in your office sometime soon?"

Teaching your children to shake hands and make eye contact is enormously helpful. Adults are bowled over by socially skilled young people. This is not meant to encourage children to be fake or manipulative. We aren't trying to create a bunch of Eddie Haskell's here (if you're under 50, look it up on YouTube). We are simply trying to point out a skill set which can benefit your children greatly if you take the time to teach it to them—one that can go a long way toward creating opportunities and resolving conflict.

Keep in Mind: Your children may need to deal with drug bullies. Young people who have chosen to use drugs can be manipulative at getting others to use with them in order to validate the decisions they have made. One of their favorite tactics is to make other children feel badly about not using. Name-calling, insults, and accusations of being on the side of the adults will be employed in their efforts to get your children to partake.

One of the critical attributes your children will need when facing the challenges of drug bullies is a sense of self-confidence and a belief in what they choose for themselves, but the ability to interact confidently with peers is next in line in importance. All these little steps that you take over the years when you teach your children how to interact socially pay great dividends when they get older and find themselves challenged by other teens who are trying to manipulate them into using drugs or drinking alcohol.

Lessons Learned: Conflict Resolution

◆ Conflict resolution is a language and social skill that lasts a lifetime.
◆ Children have a hard time figuring out why kids are mean to each other on the playground, so offer help by giving them the words and techniques to communicate with each other.
◆ Each of these concepts is a step that teaches your children to deal with people and situations that make them uncomfortable. That self-awareness gives your children the ability to say no to other kids when it comes to offers of drugs, partying, alcohol and smoking.

Using the Checklist: Conflict Resolution

☐ Am I helping my children learn how to deal with conflict?

☐ Am I listening to the problem while not letting accusations run wild?

☐ Am I making suggestions to help them without giving them the answers?

☐ Am I teaching my children to empathize with others who may be struggling with emotional difficulties?

☐ Am I teaching my child to socially engage other kids and adults?

A Final Word About Language

Keep in Mind: As you can see, language has the power to change everything. With that in mind, we want to encourage you to use the three most powerful words at your disposal as often as you can, and never miss a chance to tell your children, "I love you." Please keep communicating with them, and remember—you are not as uncool as you think you are!

Part 3

Patterns of Behavior in the Family

The following section focuses on all the little things we can do to establish patterns of behavior that help create emotionally and physically healthy children and families. Even though many of them sound like they come straight out of Hints from Heloise (that is Jonathan's cultural reference—Kelly insists she isn't old enough to know who Heloise is), they represent techniques that can help you build self-aware, confident children who have the ability to handle situations that might lead others to use drugs and alcohol. Use this section to identify what your predominant style of parenting is, and how you can use or alter that style to make the checklist best fit you and your family.

Keep in Mind: Just as we have patterns of language in our families, we also have patterns of behavior; and as with language, patterns of behavior can benefit or harm us. One of the most primary and powerful patterns of behavior we establish as parents is the style of parenting we employ; and for the majority of us, the style we find ourselves using is the one we learned from our parents. Whether we choose to follow the same path as our parents or not has a lot to do with what style or styles they used and how effective we now consider those to be. The first step is to determine what your core style is.

Establish a Pattern: What Style Parent am I?

The following basic archetypal models of parenting are based on the work of clinical and developmental psychologist Diana Baumrind. You may find that you are currently using a blend of a couple different styles; and while many psychologists encourage parents to find the right combination of styles, we need to be careful to not send mixed messages as we switch from one to another.

3.1   Archetypal Parenting Styles

♦ **The authoritarian parent** (nicknamed the military parent) expects absolute obedience to a strict set of family rules. Unfortunately, this style is associated with the highest rates of teen substance use due to the restricted lifestyle, poor social skills, low self-esteem, low self-efficacy, and rebellion found among the children of parents who employ it.

♦ **The indulgent or permissive parent** (or free for all parent) essentially allows their children to do whatever they choose. Children of these no-rules parents tend to have better social skills than those with authoritarian parents, but they also have high rates of substance use and lower levels of academic success.

♦ **The authoritative parent** (also called the child centered parent) also has a clearly defined set of rules they expect their children to follow, but the expectation of blind obedience is replaced with explanations about why the rules matter to the members of the family. There is a balance of expectation and warmth, and a high level of communication is the norm. Children of authoritative parents feel they can openly talk with their parents about challenges they face without fear of being chastised. This parenting style is associated with children who do well in school and have the lowest rate of substance abuse.

♦ **The absentee parent** (or neglectful parent) is absent for large parts of their children's lives. The cause of the absence is not necessarily the most important factor here—CEO's of Fortune 500 companies who never come home are as emotionally absent from their children's lives as are the alcoholics wasting their lives in dive bars—both are emotionally neglectful. The lack of communication, especially if it is a pattern established early in the children's lives, is associated with low academic performance, poor social skills, and high levels of substance use.

Since Dr. Spock's first book hit the shelves more than six decades and 50 million copies ago, reams of parenting advice have followed. We must now decide if we are nurturing parents, helicopter parents, slow parents, communal parents—the list is endless. Parents have to choose which style or blend of styles best suits their vision, but attention must be paid to the predicted and observed outcomes associated with their choices. We must additionally keep in mind that what works for one child may not work at all for another.

Establish a Pattern: How Do the Authors Parent?

We think it's only fair that we outline for you how we see ourselves as parents. Because we spend most of our time and most of our energy working in the field of substance abuse prevention education, it would be ridiculous and irresponsible for us to opt for any style other than the one that results in the lowest expected rate of drug and alcohol use—authoritative parenting—and yet we also see ourselves as nurturing with a touch of helicopter thrown in (which we try very hard to keep a lid on).

  The reasons we choose to parent this way are twofold: because, as we just mentioned, it is the style associated with the lowest rate of substance use; and because the parents we see who have the happiest, most well adjusted children are usually, in our observation, authoritative and nurturing. We are fortunate that our work exposes us to such a broad pool of parenting information, but we see ourselves as more fortunate to have been exposed over the years to a few spectacular parenting role models—our close friends Janey Cohen from Santa Barbara, CA, and Kerry Zarders from Long Beach, CA. Both of these women's parenting styles are marked by careful, resolute decisions expressed within a proactive, proud, authoritative mindset. Both have occasionally chosen to put their own dreams on hold in order to be sure they were attending to their children's needs first; and both made very wise choices in the men they married, which makes a world of difference when trying to present the united front discussed in Part Two. These women are the parents we aspire to be most like, and they are both inspirations for the books we write. By the way, they also have managed to raise wonderful children.

Lessons Learned: Parenting Styles

The style of parenting you employ has profound influence over what type of children you raise. Determining your style is the first step in deciding whether you need to or want to change.

Links: See links section 3A

Using the Checklist: Parenting Styles

☐ What is my predominant parenting style? Am I happy with what I find?

☐ Did I unintentionally adopt my parenting style from my parents? If so, am I OK with that?

☐ Are there any changes I could make that might put me more in line with the parent I want to be?

☐ Does my partner have the same style? If not, what can we do to make our styles more unified?

3.2   Setting Boundaries

Keep In Mind: Children thrive in an environment of reasonable, consistent rules and limits. Whether they are verbal or written, boundaries give children the confidence that the future is knowable and predictable. Children who grow up with boundaries learn structure, independence and self-awareness. By teaching your children your values, you help them learn how to make sound judgments about their behavior and to form opinions about what is right and wrong for them. Many believe that setting boundaries is one of the first steps in helping children develop their own moral compasses.

♦   We strongly recommend that one of the first boundaries you establish is that you will parent your children first, and befriend them only after you have fulfilled your duties as parents.

Establish a Pattern: Consistency

We know this sounds like a press release from the Department of Redundancy Department, but it is critical to your success as parents to establish a pattern of consistency. This does not mean that all rules and positions have to remain frozen once they are established—times, situations, and levels of emotional maturity and skill will constantly remain in flux—but it does mean that your boundaries and decisions should all source from what you currently see as the best way to keep your children safe and healthy.

Consistency requires that you explore what your beliefs and expectations are; and that you then regularly set boundaries that respect those positions. If you always call ahead when your children want to attend parties at friends' houses, you'll never have to deal with their outrage when you try to institute a call-ahead policy where none has been in effect before.

Expect difficulties if you have children who vary widely in age. We've never met a younger sibling who doesn't think it royally unfair that they aren't allowed to do exactly what the older children do, and yet that is exactly the type of situation where consistency is so useful—as children grow older and more mature, they are allowed to earn greater freedom and opportunity.

The unified front we spoke of earlier has a big role here. If all the adults who oversee your children's behavior are on the same page, you can eliminate most of the attempts by children to play one adult off of another. If mom says "No," then dad should already be understood by the children to have said "No" also—don't even bother asking. Again, this doesn't mean mom and dad will always agree, but it does mean that the disagreements over what situations elicit a negative response on the part of one parent and not the other should be worked out before hand and in private by the parents. If not, children will employ a divide and conquer strategy when they sense an opportunity.

The Words We Use: "No" is a Boundary, Consistency Will Reap its Rewards

At a 4th of July party we attended in 2011, a neighbor told us a great story about the rewards he gained from consistency. A few months earlier, his 16-year-old daughter had called him from a party and asked if she could stay for an extra hour, since it was one of the best parties she had ever attended. He explained to her that while he really appreciated the effort she made to call him, the answer was "No," and she would have to be home at her set curfew of 11pm. In the background, he could hear her friends egging her on and telling her to make up a story so she could stay out later. He knew all his hard work at staying consistent was worth it when he heard his daughter say to her friends, "No. My dad said no, and he meant it."

We know it seems like a scene out of a movie of the week, but it's just another example of the many stories we hear about kids who respond positively to and respect the boundaries their parents set. There are so many great parents out there who are building strong families by staying consistent year after year; and when their children are tempted by opportunities that the parents consider unsafe or unwise, that consistency makes it easier for them to maintain their established boundaries.

The Words We Use: Our Family Rules Travel With Us

One of our favorite moms in the world, and an excellent example of a parent who knows how to set boundaries, is Anna Lutz of Southern California. She is the mother of three amazing girls and a close friend of ours. Once, when our families were on a Disney cruise together, her two eldest daughters were justifying their request to do something by citing the fact that other kids' parent were letting their children do it. Anna's response was, "What the other families do is none of our concern. Our family rules travel with us." That statement contains such an important message—the world offers limitless opportunities and choices, but our values remain the same no matter where we are.

It's not hard to imagine that her daughters were less than pleased with her at that moment, and yet they were also very clear as to why Anna made the decision she did—it was the same decision she would have made if they were at home. It's also important to note that the limits regularly imposed by Anna have not resulted in her daughters becoming sullen, sulking, and resentful; rather they are open, bright, conversational, well-read, well-behaved, and highly accomplished. "Our family rules travel with us," is a phrase we'd like to see used more often.

Lessons Learned: Boundaries

- Boundaries help children feel secure by providing guidelines for behavior and decision-making.
- Consistency is the key—it reinforces your boundaries by establishing a pattern.
- Family rules are not place or situation dependent—they travel with you.
- Establishing firm boundaries when your children are little makes it easier for them to work within them in middle and high school.

Using the Checklist: Boundaries

☐ Am I setting boundaries, or letting my kids run all over me?

☐ Am I being consistent in my words, actions, and boundaries?

☐ Is everyone who oversees my children part of a united front?

☐ Am I sensitive to the idea that the details of the rules will change as my children grow older, but that the core values must remain consistent?

☐ Do our family rules travel with us?

3.3   Teaching Good Manners

Keep In Mind: Manners really do matter! When we teach our children good manners and how to behave in public, we are teaching them respect—not only for others, but for themselves as well. Self-respect is intimately interwoven with self-image, and both can play a huge role in your children's decisions about drugs and alcohol as they transition through the upper grades in school and into their young adult lives. Basic manners will also help with many of the situations we discussed in the language section, including social interactions with adults, teachers and peers; conflict resolution; problem solving; etc.

The Words We Use: "Is it kind?"

We credit our favorite kindergarten teacher in the world, Nancy Larimer, with instilling in our daughter her deep love of all things that relate to school. One of the simplest and yet most powerful lessons she teaches her students is that when dealing with others, always first ask the question, "Is it kind?" Our daughter, three years after leaving her class, still refers to Mrs. Larimer's Golden Rule of Kindness.

"Is it kind," can be applied in many different ways:

- Am I being kind to my best friend?
- Am I being kind to my brother?
- Am I being kind to my assistant?
- Am I being kind to the person in the checkout line?
- Am I being kind to the driver in the next lane?
- Am I being kind to my family?
- Am I being kind to my own body?
- Am I being kind in this email?

Kindness, when given and received, lowers stress and makes life more pleasant. When we teach our children the lesson of kindness, it will last them a lifetime.

Establish a Pattern: Manners

Good manners, or the lack thereof, tell others how your children were brought up, what they think of the world, and how they view themselves. Even the most basic good manners will change the way people respond to your children, and the better their manners, the better the reception they will receive socially. The basics include:

- Say "Please" and "Thank you" when requesting or receiving anything.
- Say "You're welcome" when someone thanks you.
- Say "Excuse me" if you have inconvenienced another in any way.
- Exhibit good table manners, such as chewing with your mouth closed and not sending or receiving text messages while at the table.
- Treat others with respect, even if they are functioning in a service role, such as a waiter or waitress. Teach your children that the act of performing a service does not make a person a servant.

Of course, these are just tiny examples of how your children can display good manners, but if you expand on them you create situations where your children will be much more likely to receive positive feedback, which in turn strengthens their self-confidence and self-image. Confident children who view themselves positively have much lower drug and alcohol use rates than children who lack those attributes.

Lessons Learned: Manners

Good manners lead to self-confidence, and self-confidence reduces potential drug abuse. Kindness lasts a lifetime.

Using the Checklist: Manners

☐ Am I setting a good example by using good manners?

☐ Am I encouraging and teaching my children to use good manners, and gently correcting failures to do so?

☐ Am I role modeling and teaching kindness to my children?

3.4   Establishing Patterns of Organization

Keep In Mind: We can't emphasize enough how organization reduces stress in a family. Organized children and families have lower stress levels, which can help reduce the potential that kids will use drugs and alcohol to deal with how they feel. You don't have to be Martha Stewart, but you can certainly establish patterns of organization that help your family succeed and proactively reduce stress. Remember that organization does not entail you organizing everything for your family—they have to help, too.

Being organized essentially means having what you need when you need it. For most families with children in daycare, preschool, or school, this means at a minimum you'll have organizational issues with school clothes, lunches, homework, backpacks, sports gear, and whatever else you and your children might need, like an understanding of what everyone's schedule is for the day.

Establish a Pattern: Before and After School Organization

Of the three people in our family, two of them are human tornadoes, so we have a daily system of organization that works for us. The trick is to stick to it and be consistent.

Morning Patterns: If you really want mornings to work for your children, the best thing you can do is make sure everything that can reasonably be done the night before is taken care of before your children go to bed. The rest can be done according to a schedule that is designed to suit each child's specific needs. Our daughter has a checklist of all the things she needs to do, what time she is supposed to be doing them, and a space where she can indicate she has completed the task. The checklist is printed out each week, and has five columns—one for each day. Although there is no set order you have to do things in, some items must necessarily follow others, and you should help your children arrange them in the most functional order—they may not see the flaw in a schedule that has them brushing their teeth before they eat breakfast.

Do what you need to do to make this as user-friendly for your children as you can. Our daughter loves doing her checklist; mostly because she has a collection of inked stamps she uses to mark off items she has completed. The checklist then becomes this colorful, artistic display of smiley faces, hearts, and stars as each day's tasks are completed. In the beginning, you will need to instruct your children on how to go about checking an item off. In our house, you are not allowed to check an item off if you intend to do it; it has to be completed in order to merit a stamp or check mark.

Please don't let negative, reactive thinking prevent you from trying this. We constantly hear from parents that, "There is NO WAY my child would ever do that!" Really? That's great, if your current way of doing things is running like a well-oiled machine; but most of the people we talk to recount stories of screaming, crying, fighting, driving at high speeds in a rush to get to school on time, and arriving late anyway, despite all the turmoil. The question boils down to: If what you're doing now is just torture, what have you got to lose?

If the idea of a checklist is offensive to you or your children, or if your children are too young to read, kindergarten expert and fellow mom Nancy Larimer suggests the idea of morning routine cards. Each card has a picture or drawing on it of the task to be done—a toothbrush, a hairbrush, a bowl of cereal, etc. When the task is completed, the child simply turns the card face down and moves on to the next one. If the cards are arranged in order, it becomes a checklist for pre-literate children.

Afternoon Patterns: Afternoons have their own checklist, but in our house the items on the afternoon list aren't so directly tied to a time of day. The obligations may vary from day to day, due to a variety of afternoon activities our daughter is involved in, but the core jobs that have to get done every day—homework, activities, preparation for the next day—are all on it.

Evening Patterns: Again, evenings can't all be the same due to the variety of different afternoon activities, but there will always be a group of basic obligations that have to be met. Of course, dinner is the major event of the evening, and we want to make sure to repeat the evidence that shows the power of eating dinner together as a family: If you eat dinner with your children five nights per week as opposed to just two nights per week, you cut the odds they will use alcohol, drugs, and tobacco in half. After dinner, and following whatever your family does to wind down in the early evening, the nightly obligations start to loom large. Details will vary for each child, but a loose semblance of order should be in place—your children can prepare for the next day at any time during the afternoon or evening, but of course you don't want them brushing their teeth until they are done eating for the day.

Keep in Mind: Having a pattern is not the same as living your life like a robot. If your lists assume the character of onerous jobs that must be completed in order to avoid painful consequences, your results will probably be very poor. Checklists need to be viewed as tools that help your children complete a job they want to do. If you start when your children are young and make it a fun activity, you'll probably encounter minimal resistance. If the checklist starts to cause more distress than it avoids, it might be time to look for a different way to get the job done. In the end, this is about reducing stress by getting organized. If another way works better for your children, please get in touch with us and let us know how you found success—we'll include your techniques in our follow-up publications and blogs.

Establish a Pattern: Clutter

If your goal is to get organized, clutter will defeat you and make you crazy. If you find yourself or your children searching for a piece of paper for 15 minutes before being able to file it, you may have clutter issues. Organizing your home in such a way as to minimize clutter will reduce stress and make your life more manageable.

Peter Walsh, the author of *Does This Clutter Make My Butt Look Fat?* and *It's All Too Much* said, "It's never about the stuff. There is always an underlying issue at hand." We find that eerily similar to when we say, "Drugs aren't the problem—they are a symptom of an underlying problem that isn't being dealt with in a better way." Walsh has found that too much clutter results in increased stress, and his clients often respond to that increase in stress by overeating that leads to weight problems. For our purposes, clutter causes stress, which can lead to increased drug and alcohol use. In both cases, the people being stressed are often either ignorant about its cause or blinded by denial.

We are not trying to say clutter is a direct cause of drug and alcohol abuse—we're sure there are plenty of people whose homes look like a tornado just blew through who have never used drugs or abused alcohol. It is, however, a direct cause of increased stress for many people, and that is more than enough for us to include it in this discussion. If you can take a step back for a moment and look around your home or workplace with an eye toward how much clutter you find yourself surrounded by, you may be surprised by how much mess you're standing in the middle of. If you need help, there are many professionals and organizations dedicated to getting organized, so don't be reluctant to take advantage of their assistance.

Establish a Pattern: The Color-Coded Calendar

You can't have an organized family if you don't know where everyone has to be and when they have to be there; and it can't just be mom's job to keep track of that much information in her head. We use a color-coded calendar, which is posted on the refrigerator door. If you eat or drink anything in our house, you can't help but find yourself face to face with the calendar at least six times per day. Kelly prints a monthly calendar from a Word document template she stores in a file labeled Monthly Family Calendar. We've included a sample of an average week, but since this handbook is in black and white, we should note that each person has all of their activities printed in their color. Our daughter is always in pink (the top row), Kelly is always in green (the middle row), and Jonathan is always in blue (the bottom row).

Because of the nature of our business, we can find ourselves in a new city every week; sometimes we are in multiple schools in different cities on the same day—so we list the destination school or city for each day. Appointments, special events, and activities are all listed; and we add and subtract items all the time as changes dictate. This way, at any given moment, anyone in the family will know exactly what they are supposed to be doing, but they can also easily check to see what any other member of the family is doing also. We're perfectly aware that some of you may be doubled over with laughter at the rudimentary nature of our paper scheduling, and if your PDA is synched with every other member of your family, that will work just as well or better, but we have yet to meet the family that has made the high tech solution work. Let us know if you are that family, and we'll feature you in a future publication.

Mon 2	Tues 3	Wed 4	Thurs 5	Fri 6	Sat 7
Tennis -4pm	Garden shoes	Brownies		Field trip Ballet 5pm	Sara b'day party 1pm
K – 6pm Parent mtg.	K–St. Matts	K–St. Matts J – dentist 4pm	K–St. Matts		
J – Valley	J - Valley	J - Valley	J - Valley	J - Valley	

Lessons Learned: Organization

◆ Organization reduces stress.
◆ Checklists for morning, afternoon, and evening tasks help your family get done what they need to without you having to remind them every two minutes what it is they should be doing.
◆ Clutter defeats organization and increases stress.
◆ Color-coded calendars help everyone get where they need to be and let them know where all the other members of the family are as well.
◆ Children and other family members need to be at least partly responsible for keeping track of and listing their obligations on the calendar. It can't just be mom's job to keep track of everybody.
◆ Post-it notes are excellent as reminders of what has to go where and when it has to be there.

Links: All the information on organization, charts, calendars and checklist is elaborated upon on our website: www.milestogodrugeducation.com

Using the Checklist: Organizing

☐ Do I know where my checklist is? *Yes! It's in your hand! Check it off!*

☐ Have I identified what my children need to do, when they need to do it, and put it into a checklist they can use to be responsible for their own lives?

☐ Have I addressed the issue of clutter in my life?

☐ Do I have a monthly calendar set up?

☐ Am I making sure I'm not the only one doing all the organizational work? Is my family invested into the idea of being a part of getting organized?

☐ Are we doing all we can to prepare ahead of time what we need for the next day?

☐ Are there other areas where planning could reduce stress in my life—meals, laundry, physical fitness, etc.?

3.5   I'm Bored!

Keep In Mind: "I'm bored!" is just another way for your children to say, "You're not doing your job! Entertain me!" Children who have always had someone or something to entertain them—a nanny, a parent, a video game, a TV—never develop the skill of being able to entertain themselves. The ability to entertain yourself is just like all other skills: if you practice, you get better at it. If we encourage our children to keep themselves busy by reading, drawing, playing games, doing puzzles, writing, playing or listening to music, cooking, doing science experiments, or just running around in circles, we give them a gift that will help them eliminate boredom from their lives forever.

Establish a Pattern: The Blue Bag

One of our favorite all-time anti-boredom tools is the blue bag. Of course, it doesn't have to be blue—that just happened to be the color of the left over gift bag floating around the storage area the day we needed a bag. The magic of the blue bag is that it contains about 60 slips of paper with all kinds of different activities written on them. When your children start the "I'm bored" chorus, have them get the blue bag. They are not allowed to sort through it and choose an activity; they must reach in like they are pulling out the winning ticket for a raffle and snag one of the slips of paper. There's a catch, however—they are obligated to do whatever is on the paper they randomly selected. They don't get to say they don't want that one, or get to pick another one. The reason we are so adamant about not switching activities or pulling a new piece of paper is that it forces them to do something new. If they were able to find an activity to keep themselves engaged by selecting one purposefully, they wouldn't need the blue bag, would they?

It's important to keep the bag stocked with new ideas throughout the year. Have your children think of activities to put on the slips, and every time they say they really enjoy doing something, add it to the bag. Be creative—don't just fill it with things they already do, although familiar activities are totally appropriate and should be included as a part of the mix.

Here are a few of the activities that can go in the blue bag:

♦ Shoot 25 baskets in the basketball hoop.
♦ Design an outfit in your Project Runway design book.
♦ Use the hose to wash your playhouse inside and out. *Of course, the fascination is with the hose, not the cleaning.*
♦ Swim 25 laps in the pool.
♦ Hit 50 tennis balls.
♦ Bounce the tennis ball 25 different ways, but only catch it in one hand.
♦ Read a book, just for fun, for 30 minutes.

An ever-changing and extensive list can be found on *The Mother's Checklist* section of our website. Please send us your blue bag ideas so we can share them with other parents.

Lessons Learned: Boredom and the Blue Bag

There is always something to do—you just have to have a blue bag. It's all about thinking ahead and being organized.

Using the Checklist: Boredom and the Blue Bag

☐ Do I have a blue bag?

☐ Did I add anything new to the blue bag this month?

3.6   Over-Programming vs. The Quiet Mind

Keep In Mind: Some kids are highly stressed simply because they are over-programmed. If your children have something scheduled every minute of every day, they are prime candidates for burnout. For parents who both work, it is often hard to just take some time off on the weekends. Parents who work long hours may feel like they haven't spent enough quality time with their children, so they load up the weekends with dozens of activities designed to pack as much time together as possible. Time together is great—it builds strong bonds parents and children so often lack. It's just as important to realize, though, that every minute doesn't have to be spent doing something specific—sometimes it's just as rewarding for both parents and children to slow down and take a deep breath.

Another problem with being constantly scheduled is it teaches children they must be constantly stimulated. The ability to be quiet, to wait for things rather than to be immediately gratified, is an important skill for children (and their parents) to develop.

Establish a Pattern: Quieting the Mind

The human brain is designed to be hyper-vigilant. We are built so we can respond to a threat almost instantaneously, either by fighting or fleeing—the classic fight or flight response. It used to be that stressors were short duration events—either the saber tooth tiger ate us or it didn't. Soon after the stress was gone, so was the response to it. We freaked out, and then we calmed down. Today, stress is an almost constant state of existence for a lot of people, and the toll it exacts upon us is equally constant—unless we learn how to counter it.

If we can teach our children at an early age how to relax, how to quiet their minds when they start to race, we can inoculate them against the negative consequences of ongoing, unrelenting stress—heart disease, psychiatric illnesses, cancer, and drug and alcohol abuse. Self-medicating to deal with the symptoms of stress has become a national crisis, but it is a crisis with a treatment. We owe it to our children to teach them how to deal with negative stress.

The good news is that methods that help us deal with the negative effects of stress are readily available:

102

- Tai chi, yoga, massage, and meditation can help with balance, flexibility and quieting the mind.
- We use sound machines, fountains, and what we call "the baby music"—soft jazz we played constantly when our daughter was a baby to help soothe her in the car—to mitigate the stress caused by the noise pollution we are surrounded by almost constantly.
- Many families will put quiet days on their calendars. A simple, pre-planned meal, a movie or a board game, and everyone lounging in their pajamas are wonderful ways to spend a relaxing evening. Candles, soft music and a hot tub are great too—remember that moms need their own stress reduction.
- The Crane School in Santa Barbara sets aside time each day after lunch called SSR—sustained silent reading. It's one of the most amazing things to see: hundreds of young people reading in almost complete silence. You can do this in your home as well; just set aside a mere quarter hour each day following a meal during which everyone does something relaxing, refreshing and rejuvenating.
- One really good way to reduce stress is to not create it in the first place. Julie Byrd, a really smart mom we know, limits her daughter to a maximum of three activities outside school at any given time. Over-scheduling is a demon that can be dealt with, but it requires us to sometimes make hard choices and prioritize our desires.

Lessons Learned: Over-Programming vs. The Quiet Mind

Periods of down time are essential for a balanced life. Kids don't need to have everything handed to them immediately or do everything they want to do all at once. Parents need to teach their children that being together is an important part of being a family; everyone doesn't have to be on the go all the time. Help your children learn to prioritize their wishes, and to delay some things until later in order to avoid burning them out.

Using the Checklist: Over-Programming vs. The Quiet Mind

☐ Are we over-programmed this month?

☐ Have I found a way for my kids to quiet their brains without being bored?

☐ Have I assessed every person's individual need to have a down day?

☐ Have I scheduled a quiet day?

☐ Did I put SSR on the calendar?

3.7 Chunk It Down

Keep in Mind: As adults, most of us can take a large task and break it down into smaller, identifiable, manageable pieces. Our children, especially in the earliest grades in school, have much greater difficulty identifying the size and scope of a task. To a first grader, everything is big; and it can be hard for them to get a handle on how to get a task like homework started and completed. If a job looks too big or overwhelming, it's easy to see how that job could add stress to a child's life; and if we don't teach our children how to break tasks into smaller chunks, we may be dooming them to a lifetime of feeling overwhelmed and stressed.

The Words We Use: "Clean up your room," vs. "Find 10 things to put away."

For some kids, cleaning up their rooms can be a daunting task; not because the job itself is so gargantuan, but because they have no idea of how to begin or end it—in fact, they may not even be able to conceive that it will ever end. When people see a task as undoable, or when they fear they will not do it well, they can avoid failure and ridicule by putting off starting it. This, for so many people, is the root cause of procrastination—if they never start the job, they can never fail at it. You can work around this problem with your children by defining the scope of the task in the context of your request to do it. Instead of saying, "Clean up your room," ask your children instead to, "Pick up and put away 10 things in your room."

Obviously, some children will initially try to game the system by using your words literally as opposed to figuratively—they will insist they have met their obligation by picking up 10 pieces of the puzzle that is scattered all over their bedroom floor. It may take a while to establish that the puzzle is one thing, not dozens or hundreds as represented by the pieces of the puzzle itself. This phase should pass quickly, once they understand their trick isn't going to work. Some kids might even need you to kick-start the process in the beginning. You can accompany them to their rooms, point to any item that needs attention, and say, "Put your toy on that shelf, where it belongs." When they have done so, congratulate them with, "Good job! That's one—only nine more to go."

What if picking up 10 things doesn't even make a dent in the job of cleaning up your children's rooms? That's where the idea of breaking tasks into smaller pieces—chunking it down—comes into play. If you break a large task into smaller pieces and separate those pieces with fun activities your children want to do, you will eliminate or seriously reduce their resistance to doing the job. If you separate five sessions of picking up 10 things by inserting a quick, fun activity in between each session, you will have helped your children pick up 50 things with relatively little effort on your part.

Establish a Pattern: Chunk it Down

Homework is an area where chunking it down can make everyone's lives more pleasant and easier to manage. As an example, let's say your 3rd grade daughter has homework that consists of one page of math problems, 20 minutes of reading, and 10 spelling words to practice. It's easy for us to forget that our children's lives are as busy and hectic as ours are. Even a third grade student can be worn out by the time they finally get home from school, and the last thing many of them want to do is plop down at a desk and do more school work at the end of that long day. You can make it so much more user-friendly by just breaking it into pieces—all you need is a good kitchen timer and a few activities. If you can find a timer that has a fun theme or a really interesting sound, so much the better—ours is a Donald Duck timer that you set by twisting the head. Now all our exemplary 3rd grader has to do is chunk it down:

- ◆ Upon her return from school, she puts her backpack in its appropriate place and then washes her hands.
- ◆ She removes her homework folder or binder from her pack and takes it to her desk or designated homework area.
- ◆ She identifies what has to be done, either by arranging her papers in order or checking her homework agenda she created at school that day.
- ◆ She establishes, with your help if necessary at first, what order she wants to do her work in, and identifies that order either by creating a checklist or by putting Post-its at the top of each page.
- ◆ Now that she is organized and has everything she needs laid out, this is a good time for the first break. Set the timer for five

106

minutes, 10 if she is going to have a snack. She may now jump on the trampoline, do 25 cartwheels, etc. A healthy snack will also give her energy and eliminate any hunger pangs that may distract her once she starts her work.

- The instant the timer rings, the activity stops and the homework starts. This has to be clear—there can be no "I just want to finish this level in my video game" or any delay of that sort. When the bell goes off, it's time to start work.
- The next break period is earned by completing the first chunk of homework correctly and neatly. Rushing pell-mell through the work in order to go back to playing should result in her having to redo the work until it is up to standard. The break is a reward for doing it well, not doing it fast.
- When the first section of homework is complete, set the timer again for the second break, and continue this pattern until everything is finished. You can vary the time allotted for the breaks—if you find five minutes just isn't long enough, make it 10 instead. Whatever works for you is what's most important, and if the solution causes more problems than it fixes, it isn't a solution at all.
- When everything is done, make sure to follow your organizational guidelines set up earlier. Homework, once finished, goes in the backpack for the next day; and the backpack is placed where it is supposed to be so it can be grabbed the next day with no confusion or wild searching.

Chunking it down works with all large tasks—household chores, yard work, etc. It will lower everyone's stress level by eliminating most of the back and forth struggle so many parents go through as they battle with their children over what to do, when to do it, and how it should be done. It will establish a pattern of behavior at a young age that will improve the quality of your children's lives as well as that of those around them.

Lessons Learned: Chunk it Down

Almost every job will appear unpleasant if it is perceived out of proportion. By chunking it down, you right-size it and make it manageable. Quality of life is increased and stress is decreased when you break big jobs into smaller pieces.

Using the Checklist: Chunk it Down

☐ What tasks in my home might benefit from being broken down into smaller pieces?

☐ Do my children know how to chunk down their homework? Their chores?

☐ Do I have Post-its scattered freely about so my family can organize their work?

☐ Do I have a list of fun things to do in between the work?

3.8   Establishing Passion

Keep in Mind: Finding the balance point between when to push your children to do something because it is good for them and when to stop pushing because you are doing them harm is one of the most difficult obligations parents face. The problem: for every person who talks about how much they hate this or that because their parents forced them to do it, there is another who insists that, even though they hated every minute of this or that, their life is so much richer now because their parents insisted they continue.

Establish a Pattern: Push or Passion?

There is no right answer here. It would appear that what has served us in other areas we have explored will be equally likely to serve us here; in other words, nurturing and authoritative parents will set guidelines for their children according to what they see as being best for them while they also constantly talk about how things are going and how their children feel. The last thing we want is resentful, depressed children slogging their way through a nightmare of passionless obligations simply because their parents insist they do so; but neither do we want hazy, unfocused ditherers who flit from one activity to the next and never achieve more than a surface understanding of a subject or skill.

One question you might ask of yourself is, "Am I pushing them for them, or am I pushing them for me?" Is it your dream or theirs you're trying to realize? If you find that the activity in question is driving a wedge between you and your children, it may be time to reassess where to direct your energies.

The other side of the issue is equally hard for parents to process—when they find the activities their children are deeply passionate about to be a waste of time or patently useless. The issue is usually the degree of immersion in the activity the child is experiencing. Video games are not evil per se, but children who play them for hours and hours every day are being detrimentally affected by them. That said, however, teenagers who play certain video games are measurably more accurate manipulators of surgical robots than are the surgeons who use them for real. Who can say when today's seemingly useless passion becomes tomorrow's high tech job opportunity?

If you are interested in finding your children's passions, we highly recommend *The Element* by Ken Robinson, Ph.D. On his website, Sir Robinson defines the element as "the point at which natural talent meets personal passion." This is a must-read for parents who despair over whether their children will ever discover their passion, and it is packed with positive language your children should hear as they explore the world in pursuit of their passion.

The Words We Use: A Great Quote

"When you push anyone, including a child, to do anything, you create resistance – even if it started out as something they originally wanted to do. It is better to invite and encourage from a feeling of caring or love than to push. The results will be much more productive." *Hale Dwoskin, CEO and Director of Training, Sedona Training Associates*

Lessons Learned: Push or Passion

Parents walk a fine line in determining when and how hard to push their children. The old saying used to be, "Practice makes perfect." Today's understanding is that, "Practice makes permanent. Only perfect practice makes perfect." That's a lot of stress to put on children, especially in light of the added understanding that practice doesn't make people passionate.

Using the Checklist: Passion

☐ Am I pushing my children to do something they don't want to do?

☐ Is it my dream or my child's dream?

☐ Can I help my children find their passions?

☐ Did we try something new this month?

☐ Have I accidentally driven a wedge between me and my child by pushing?

☐ Do my children enjoy the activities they are doing?

3.9 Outlining Your Family Values

Keep In Mind: When you actively discuss your family's values with your children, you equip them with a set of expectations and beliefs that travels with them wherever they go. Many parents we meet, though, think their children will somehow magically understand these things without ever actually discussing them. If you have ever found yourself beginning a sentence with the words, "It should go without saying…" you may want to visit the idea of outlining your family values. As you do this, you should also consider an additional step—writing them down.

It is not our intention that you create some flowery corporate document. Nothing requires that it be full of big words or printed on heavy vellum and professionally framed—it can take any of a hundred forms. The important thing is that it says who you are and what you believe as a family. It's also best if it is in a form that can be constantly modified and added to. As your needs and situations change, this document can change with them. As an example, we don't feel it's necessary to talk to four and five year olds about abusing drugs, but you can certainly talk about honesty, healthy eating, etc. As your children get older, though, your discussions definitely need to address the issues of drug and alcohol use, and those can then be added to the family values statement.

The Words We Use: How to Be a Scott

Some of you may have already caught on to the fact that we are actually discussing the creation of a family mission statement. Unfortunately, there are few faster ways to send your children screaming into the woods than to invite them to have a seat and create a family mission statement with you. It is for that reason we recommend you not call it that—ever. A few years ago, a very wise parent realized this and shared with us her family's method of exploring their values and writing them down without uttering the poisoned phrase.

She explained that her family simply tapes a huge piece of poster paper to the refrigerator door. On it, they write what it is exactly that makes their family unique; essentially, what it means to be one of them. They titled the paper, "How to be a Smith." On it, they then wrote what behaviors and beliefs qualified a person for membership in the Smith family. The example she used was that everyone in her family loved chicken and dumplings; so the first entry at the top was, "In order to be a Smith, you MUST love chicken and dumplings." As the years went by and their lives got more complicated, the entries became more earnest, but she was quick to point out that they never forgot to include a bit of humor. Every once in a while, someone would write down a lighthearted observation of what it meant to be a Smith.

Below, we have an example of a few of the entries on our values poster:

How to Be a Scott:

1. If you want to be a Scott, you have to eat healthy, unprocessed foods most of the time.
2. The Scott family LOVES In-n-Out Hamburgers! *(As you can see, there is wiggle room.)*
3. To be a Scott, you should be a fan of exercising regularly.
4. The Scott family believes in honesty.
5. If you want to be a Scott, you can't abuse drugs and alcohol.
6. Smoking tobacco is cause for instant dismissal from family membership!
7. The Scott family believes in redemption—you can rejoin the family if you promise to never smoke again!
8. The Scott family LOVES school!
9. To be a Scott, you have to have goals—and a plan to achieve them.

Establish a Pattern: Your Family Mission Statement

♦ Find some way to outline and write down your family values.
♦ All family members need to be involved in creating this document. Input from the whole family is critical to everyone investing in it.
♦ Children and parents should agree that family values don't change at the front door—they travel with you wherever you go.

Recommended Reading:

♦ Shameless Plug #761—our first book, *Not All Kids Do Drugs*, discusses family mission statements in Section Two.

♦ In *7 Habits for Highly Effective Families*, Stephen Covey discusses family mission statements extensively.

♦ *Your Family Constitution, A Modern Approach to Family Values and Household Structure*, by Scott Gale, is an easy to read manual on how to set up a family mission statement.

♦ *How to Behave So Your Preschoolers Will Too*, by Sal Severe, says, "When you talk about your values and goals, your children will come to you with their problems. This will come in handy when they are teenagers." Dr. Severe's books are terrific, and we especially like his Top 10 Parenting Tips, which can be found at http://www.howtobehave.com/topten.html.

Lessons Learned: Family Mission Statements

We know—the words "family mission statement" make your head hurt—but please don't dismiss this because it sounds hard. If you want your children to know what your family values are, you will have to identify and state what they are. This is best done in writing, but it does not have to be overly complex or ornate. Children should actively participate in the creation of your family values statement.

Using the Checklist: Outlining Your Family Values

☐ Have we outlined our family values?

☐ Have we created a document that represents our family mission statement?

☐ Do we need to update it?

☐ Is it easy to view and edit for all members of the family?

3.10 Setting Goals

Keep in Mind: Setting goals is a critical skill for children to master. In *Life Strategies for Teens*, Jay McGraw interviewed hundreds of teens, and one of the most important questions he asked was why each of them had chosen to do or not do drugs. The teenagers who had not done drugs said they didn't because drug use either didn't fit their plans or interfered with important goals they were working toward. The teens who did use drugs said they did it because they were bored and there was no compelling reason not to—in other words, they didn't have any goals.

Establish a Pattern: Personal Goals and Delayed Gratification

There are so many books and websites dedicated to setting and achieving goals that it must now be considered a cottage industry. Why then, are so many of us so bad at setting and realizing goals? For many of us, it's because goals equal pressure to perform, and one thing we don't need is more pressure and stress in our lives. Add to that the fact that a lot of people fail when they set goals—how many New Year's Resolutions do you think are broken by February? Certainly most, and yet who likes to see oneself as a failure? But goals can also open up whole new worlds of achievement and happiness for us, especially if we learn to view them positively and develop the skills necessary to use them for benefit and gain.

The great thing about goals is that they fit so well with the ideas discussed in family mission statements. If your children have a material goal they want to reach—the purchase of a particular CD, say—you certainly don't want them to steal the money to buy it; and so goals become exercises in laying out the paths by which your children will achieve them.

Another positive aspect of goals is that they teach children to delay gratification, a skill that is way more important than it first seems. At the time of this handbook's publication, scientists had recently revisited the subjects of a landmark study on delayed gratification. In the study, the researchers observed the behaviors of children when they were offered a choice: immediately consume a marshmallow, or wait a few minutes and receive a second marshmallow as a reward for waiting.

The children who waited possessed the ability to delay gratification. As the researchers followed the test subjects into their teens, they found that the children who resisted temptation had better self-images, higher levels of self-efficacy, scored higher on their SAT's, and had better relationships with their peers and parents.

The most recent assessment of the test subjects revealed dramatic results. The children who lacked the ability to delay gratification grew up to be adults with the same lack of control, and they also expressed multiple problems associated with impulse control—gambling addiction, drug and alcohol addiction, weight problems, and trouble saving for retirement.

The studies on impulse control have revealed actual physical differences in the brains of the two most widely varying forms— high delay and low delay. We must now figure out if we can override the neurological predisposition to succumb to impulse by establishing patterns that allow our children to practice delayed gratification. It would seem, since we generally won't have the slightest idea of what our individual children's brain structures are, that the best path is the one that teaches and builds skills that make our children better able to delay gratification. If our children happen to be high delayers, we will build upon their strengths; if they are low delayers, we can mitigate the predisposition they have to respond to impulse—or at least that would be our hope.

The Words We Use: "Let's put it on your dream board."

Writing down goals and setting paths and timetables to realize them is certainly beyond the skill set of younger children, especially if they can't read or write yet, but that doesn't mean they can't learn how to set goals and delay gratification. In this case, a picture can substitute for written goals.

In our house, we use what is called a dream board. The dream board is just a picture collage of images that represent goals and desires our daughter has. When she was three or four, two of her goals were to learn to whistle and learn how to snap her fingers. We did an image search online, found pictures of fingers snapping and lips pursed to whistle, printed them out and pinned them to the dream board. When a goal is realized, the picture is removed and replaced with a new one, and even though our daughter is now perfectly capable of writing her goals down, she still uses the dream board as a way to remind herself what she is working toward. Today, her dream board is covered with images of Disney cruise ships, purses, CD's, and shoes. As goals are realized, we put the old pictures in a file, as we are sure it will be fun to go back and look at them years from now. As an alternative, you might want to leave all the pictures on the board, and watch as goals are realized and your children build a map of where they were and how far they have come.

Lessons Learned: Goals

Teaching your children to set goals should be high on your list of goals. Setting goals is a critical skill that adds benefit and capacity to your children's entire lives; and it is a skill which can begin even before your children can read or write. When your children express a desire for something, it's a great idea to create a delay by setting a goal via the dream board.

Links: See links section 3B

Using the Checklist: Goal Setting

☐ Do you have a goal or dream board for yourself?

☐ Do your children have goal or dream boards for themselves?

☐ Can you identify three ways you helped your child delay gratification this month?

☐ Have you seen successes, big or small, to remind you that your family goals are working?

3.11 Yelling and Hitting

Keep in Mind: For most psychologists and professionals who work with children, yelling and hitting have been relegated to the dustbin of bad methods for building healthy, emotionally sound children. Unfortunately, they are both behaviors many parents have historically employed, and they continue to perpetuate as the children who are yelled at and hit carry that legacy forward by doing the same to their kids. Children living in homes where yelling and hitting are the norm live in states of fear and chaos that make them feel they have no control over their situations.

If your children were about to step into the path of a speeding car, you would be perfectly justified in screaming at the top of your lungs, "Stop!" If your children were about to insert their hands into the open top of a running blender, you would be irresponsible to not slap their hands away. In situations like these, feelings of fear and concern for your children's safety are motivating your actions, and yelling and hitting play a critical role in keeping your children safe. In most cases where parents yell at and strike their children, however, different emotions are at play. Everyone experiences anger and frustration from time to time, and letting those feelings fester by not dealing with them is unhealthy. If, however, you deal with feelings of anger or frustration by hitting your children or yelling at them, you have officially lost control and need to step back, take a deep breath, and consider other options.

Remember, there is a huge difference between yelling and raising your voice. We regularly raise our voices in our home. After a long day, when we find ourselves lounging on the couch watching TV, we may find we want our daughter to come out to the living room. The problem is, neither of us wants to get up and go get her; so what we do is call her name really loudly until she comes. If she has music on in her room, we may have to really belt it out before she hears. When she does, she comes out to see what we want, but she is in no way scared or intimidated by the volume of our voices. What is completely lacking is the tone of anger, which would transform our raised voices into yelling if it were present. A raised voice that lacks the intent to intimidate or express anger does not constitute yelling.

Establish a Pattern: Stop Yelling

On the episode of the Dr. Phil show titled *Fighting in Front of the Kids*, Phil McGraw had two quotes of extraordinary power: "When you fight with each other in front of your children, you forever change who they are," and, "Fighting in front of your kids is nothing short of abuse." You don't just do damage when you yell at your kids, you also cause harm when you yell in front of them.

In addition to the fact that yelling is damaging to your children, it also creates a cycle that ensures you will have to continue to yell once you start—if you raise your voice consistently in order to get what you want, you teach your children that your words have no meaning until you yell them. You do not gain respect when you yell, you lose it.

The Words We Use: "I'm tired of yelling, and I'm not going to do it anymore."

It is just that simple—if you want to stop yelling, you have to decide that is what you want. If you have been yelling for a long time, it's going to take your children a while to figure out how to deal with the new you. This will require that when you say something, you say it once, you say it in a normal tone of voice, and if nobody listens to you they will have to pay the price for that choice.

If, in the past, you have yelled "Dinner!" countless times, only to have your children ignore you until you are yelling so loudly you have veins standing out on your forehead, you can't expect that they will come the first time you calmly say to each of them, "Dinner is ready. Please come eat now." Whether they come eat is now up to them. You, however, should sit down and enjoy whatever it is you prepared, even if you are completely alone as you do so. When you are finished, clear the table, wrap up what's left over, and put it in the fridge.

When your children eventually wonder why you aren't screaming your brains out, or when they realize they are starving, they will wander in and ask what's for dinner. Depending on their ages, you can tell them where it is and invite them to enjoy it as a cold meal or reheat it if they know how to, or you can take it out and offer it to your younger children cold. This is not going to go well

119

the first time you do it, and you should expect some wailing and crying—that's normal. What you cannot do is give in to it and start re-preparing dinner for each of your children as they straggle in— that will surely reinforce the notion that you don't mean what you say until you scream it. Calmly explain to them, "I told you dinner was ready, and you didn't listen. In the future, if you want to enjoy dinner while it is warm, you'll come when I ask. I'm tired of yelling, and I'm not going to do it anymore."

If you commit yourself to not yelling, and follow through with consequences for the times when your children choose to ignore you, you will find that your children will eventually realize they have to listen to you when you speak, not when you yell. If you regularly find yourself on the verge of yelling, it may help if you verbalize how it is that you feel and what you are going to do to deal with it. If your children do something that in the past would have elicited a screaming match, calmly say, "I'm going to take a deep breath and wait for you to rethink your behavior."

Please understand, we are not advocating some sort of 60's hippie commune response to bad or abusive behavior. It is not OK for children to misbehave or disrespect their parents, and they should understand that there are always consequences for the choices they make. The point here is that yelling only causes people to react negatively. They will either be afraid of you, ignore you, or start yelling back at you, and all of those are bad outcomes.

We have found that, given the chance, most children will do the right thing if they are shown what the right thing is; and most children dearly love their parents, but have forgotten how to say or show that because of all the yelling that has been going on for so long. On the rare occasions when, out of some frustration or misunderstanding, our daughter says something unkind or rude to us, all we have to do is calmly ask, "Is that really the way you want to treat me? Would you like to take a moment to think that over and see if you'd rather say it differently?" She has never failed to come back, be it within a few seconds or a few minutes, and apologize. Usually, she will explain why she felt the way she did—how frustration or fatigue drove her to say something she didn't mean— and nobody has to yell in order for this to happen.

Establish a Pattern: Stop Hitting

Since we're on a Dr. Phil kick, let's cite him once more, this time about spanking: "When you raise your hand to a child, you teach them to disregard your words." It's ultimately the same dynamic as yelling—if you teach your children that you don't mean what you say until you start swinging, they won't do what you say until you hit them. Hitting is doubly damaging, though, since you are now inflicting physical as well as emotional damage. Spanking also translates very poorly into your children's skill sets, since you teach them that they can get what they want by hitting other children. How on earth are our children supposed to listen when we tell them to "use your words" when we use our hands or other weapons to physically intimidate them when we want them to behave a certain way?

We understand that you don't have to look very far to find tons of people who still advocate spanking as a means of raising children and teaching them to obey, but we choose to respectfully disagree. Not only has physical abuse by parents been shown in a multitude of studies to do all kinds or psychological damage to children, but it is also sometimes very hard to keep a lid on the intensity of the violence once you start dishing it out. We are fully convinced that very few of the parents who beat their children so severely that they either end up in the hospital or the morgue intended that as an outcome when they first raised their hands to their children. If you do hit your children, have you ever found yourself frightened when your anger got out of control and the violence escalated to a level you never imagined it would when you began? If not, maybe you're lucky, so far. If you have, how could you ever raise your hand to them again, knowing what you do?

This all comes back to the patterns we have talked about so extensively—if your pattern is to respond to your children with violence when they misbehave, you will do so both when you are mildly irritated and when you are enraged. When a human mind achieves a state of true rage, it has lost the ability to meter its responses to the world. We wonder how many parents find themselves abusing drugs or alcohol as they try to erase the haunting memories of losing control and physically abusing their children. Additionally, we wonder how many children end up abusing drugs

121

and alcohol as a result of the abuse they endured at the hands of their parents. Discipline by physical abuse is just a bad deal all the way around. Take a deep breath. Use your words. And get help if you find you can't do either when you should.

Lessons Learned: Yelling and Hitting

Yelling and spanking hurt your children. If you find yourself doing either, find a way to change the dynamic in your family. If you don't, you are essentially creating another generation of yellers and abusers who will then pass their behaviors on to their children. You owe it to your children, and your children's children, to stop.

Links: See links section 3C

Using the Checklist: Yelling and Hitting

☐ Am I currently a yeller or a spanker?

☐ Do I want to find new ways to achieve my goals?

☐ What areas of my life currently need adjustment, and how can I create a plan to get that done?

☐ Have I practiced taking a deep breath before yelling lately?

☐ How can I institute consequences for my children's negative behaviors without hitting them?

☐ Do I know how to get help if I need it?

3.12 Laughter

Keep in Mind: One of the greatest gifts we can give our children is the freedom to laugh. To hear a child let loose a wild, unrestrained peal of laughter is a gift of unimaginable value. The old quote about laughter being the best medicine has been shown to be accurate, at least to the extent that it is good for your health.

People who laugh a lot are healthier, have less stress, and worry less than those who grumble their way through life. Knowing how to laugh is not just about having a good sense of humor, though. Children should also be taught how to laugh at themselves. None of us is going to get through this world without doing something incredibly silly and embarrassing, so if you can laugh at the situation—laugh at your essential humanity—you will be able to forgive yourself the *faux pas* and move on. Children who can laugh at themselves can move on after they make mistakes, and they have lower levels of stress than the children who suffer the agony of replaying embarrassments over and over in their minds.

Establish a Pattern: Laugh at Yourself

Teach your children the art of laughing at themselves the same way you do everything else—by doing it yourself. One of the main reasons children feel embarrassed when they do something silly is because they think they are the only person it has ever happened to. If you can highlight the goofy mistakes you make, or tell a story at dinner about some alarmingly boneheaded move you made that day, and do it with smiles and laughter, you will teach your children to do the same. In our family, whenever anyone realizes they are being a doofus, they look to the rest of the family and ask, "How do you spell spazz?" The rest of the family gleefully answers by spelling the name of the person in question. In our family, we relish opportunities to laugh at ourselves.

Lessons Learned: Laughter

This is the most enjoyable thing you will do in this whole book—lighten up, and get a good chuckle at the hilarity of being human. Life is just too hard not to.

Using the Checklist: Laughter

☐ Are we laughing as a family?

☐ Am I teaching my kids to laugh at themselves?

☐ Can we laugh through adversity?

☐ Can we find something funny about struggling through a problem?

3.13 The Internet

Keep in Mind: Even with content filters, spam blockers, password protection, and anti-virus programs, the Internet is still the electronic equivalent of the Wild West. Without parental oversight, the Internet can be as dangerous to your children as a predator lurking outside their bedroom window. Most schools are protected adequately enough that you don't have to worry a lot about what your children will be exposed to on campus computers, but smart phones, touch pads, laptops and home desktops need to be overseen if we are to do all we can to keep our children safe, technologically speaking.

A number of studies have shown that children today are pretty good at protecting themselves online, but pretty good doesn't cut it when it come to the safety of our children. Not only do parents need to monitor the content of the websites, chat rooms, and social media sites their children visit, they need to stay on top of email and various messaging services as well. Children aren't as savvy as they sometimes think they are, and they can be easily misled by an official looking website telling them drug and alcohol use is perfectly safe for kids; or by a predator posing as a friendly peer. As parents, we have to learn a little bit every day in order to stay as up to speed as we can to protect our children on the high tech front lines.

Establish a Pattern: Internet Rules

Here are a few key tips that we've learned from parents and the experts:

1. Internet access in your home should be communal. There shouldn't be any closed doors between you and your children when they are online.
2. Parents should keep all cell phones, touch pads, etc. in their bedroom when bedtime rolls around. There is no good reason for a teenager to have a cell phone in their bedroom when they are supposed to be sleeping.
3. Take a class or workshop, somewhere, anywhere, on how to keep your children safe on the Internet. We have a friend who

hunts down cyber-predators, and his descriptions of his prey are bone chilling.

4. Keep in mind that the Internet is your children's information lifeline. Despite the risks, it is vital that our children learn how to use the vast amount of information on the Internet to their benefit.

Lessons Learned: The Internet

The Internet is the perfect double-edged sword—it is rich with information while being equally filled with misinformation and risk.

Using the Checklist: The Internet

☐ What are my children seeing on the Internet? Am I taking time to monitor their use?

☐ Am I asking questions about what they are researching online?

☐ Are we learning how to cross-check research so that we aren't accepting one point of view?

☐ Are we collecting electronics every night to eliminate their use in the middle of the night?

☐ Am I warning my kids that the comments that follow an article online are not part of the scientific research or the article?

3.14 Establishing Patterns Outside the Home

Keep In Mind: How your children conduct themselves outside of your home environment will become more and more important as they get older. You don't really need to worry as much about what goes on at the birthday party of a six-year-old as you do about what happens at an unsupervised party packed with teenagers. Staying aware of what your children are up to is harder when they get older, but it is no less critical. The patterns you establish when they are young will keep you actively engaged in their lives when they are older.

Establish a Pattern: Calling Ahead

Whenever your children are outside your direct supervision, the most critical factor that can ensure their safety is the supervision of another responsible adult. After school sports have coaches and assistants to fill that role, the dance studio has the instructors and the managers, and pools have lifeguards. When your children are visiting friends, hopefully the parents of those friends will fill in for you, but that isn't always the case, especially if the social event at the time is a party. Whenever your children visit the home of another family, you need to call ahead (or be comfortable enough with the other parents' values as to not have to) to make sure exactly what will be going on and who will be supervising the gathering. Unsupervised teenagers are nothing more than a recipe for disaster.

As we noted earlier, we are currently in the process of creating a handbook called *Where's the Party?* In it, we will detail all the steps you can take to stay on top of your teenagers' social lives when it comes to parties and social events in middle and high school. The basic issue, though, will always boil down to supervision.

Establish a Pattern: Supervision

Children who are supervised don't get into as much trouble as those who aren't. We're not even going to provide a footnote for that one—that's teenage troublemakers 101. So how do you make sure your children are properly supervised as continuously as possible?

Here are a few suggestions:

- As we said, call ahead.
- If children are in your house, you need to be there and be aware. Let them know you are watching.
- Start chaperoning your children's parties when they are really young, and don't stop. There are two types of parents when it comes to kids' parties—the ones who drop off and the ones who stay. Now, we understand that it isn't desirable or feasible to have every parent present at every party, but you should at least be a regular in the rotation of parents who chaperone their children's social events. When you join the group of parents who stay, you form friendships and start to build a trust that your children are safe with them and theirs are with you as well. Some of the best friends we have today are people we met as we sat through the countless birthday, Halloween, and back-to-school parties we are obligated to attend as parents. Also, when you stay, you train your kids to expect your presence at their parties. This is going to make it a lot easier to walk into parties they attend as teenagers; and if you wait until your children are teenagers before you start this, you've waited too long.
- One of our dear friends (and a great mom), Lisa Argyros, does something really smart—she invites us to chaperone her teens' parties. Not a lot of drugs and alcohol get used when the party is chaperoned by "The Drug Guys."

Establish a Pattern: Don't Get Drunk in Front of Your Kids

You can be a role model for your children if you drink alcohol in moderation at home or at social events, as long as you don't drive afterward. If you follow the recommendations for moderate drinking, i.e. one drink per day for women and two drinks for men, you will show your children how to behave moderately around alcohol in adulthood. If, however, you insist on getting drunk, you immediately step over into the area of inappropriate role modeling. In our opinion, your children really don't need to see you drunk, ever. It's not that we don't understand that lots of people like how it feels when they are intoxicated, but it's really not a great idea for

128

you to model getting ripped for your kids. If you're going to do it, do it when your kids aren't around.

Establish a Pattern: Safe Homes Agreements

A number of communities have instituted what are called safe home agreements or social host party agreements. Parents who sign them are making a statement that they will not provide or allow the use of drugs or alcohol at any function they have at their home or that they chaperone. We have mixed feelings about communities that coerce parents into cooperating—if you are forced to sign something of this nature when you don't agree with it or support it, all the other people who signed it can't tell who actually believes in it and who signed because they had to. If, however, you can assemble a group of parents who willingly agree they will provide safe party environments for children who visit their homes, you can create a team of like-minded parents you feel safe leaving your kid in the care of. You can find a list of model cities and their agreements on our website at *www.milestogodrugeducation.com.*

Lessons Learned: Supervision

Supervision is critical when it comes to keeping your children safe when they are outside your care. Call ahead, network, and chaperone when your children attend parties. Start when they are young, and continue to do so during their teen years.

Using the Checklist: Patterns Outside the Home

☐ Am I calling ahead when my children attend social events? *Remember, this sets up a pattern for later.*

☐ Have I offered to chaperone a party?

☐ Have I started a network of parents to rely on for parties?

☐ Am I offering to help at all the different parties my children attend?

☐ Have I started a Safe Homes agreement at my school?

3.15 Establishing Your Goals; Taking Care of You

Keep In Mind: Even though you want to, and even though everyone seems to think you should, you cannot do it all! If you don't learn to make time for yourself, and establish in the minds of your family that you need to do so, you may find yourself having helped everyone else reach their goals while completely failing to reach your own. Your dreams do not belong in the back seat, and neither do you. You have to firmly but lovingly insist that every member play a role in your family's success. In the beginning, as you start down this path, in order to let them know what it is that they should be doing to facilitate that goal, you may find that you have to make everyone a list. You cannot carry everyone's life path in your head—there isn't enough room for all that and your dreams and goals at the same time.

Establish a Pattern: Make Lists

Until they learn how to do it for themselves, make lists for the members of your family. If you are currently doing it all, you have to let go of some of the things you are doing. Your husband can go to the grocery store—they have big signs on them so he can easily find them. Your children can help you get dinner ready. Yes, we know it's easier if you just do it yourself, but that's only true in the beginning. If you can teach your family how to prepare food, they can do the whole job themselves as they get older. Isn't it a lot easier if someone else does it all? They can, if you teach them and hold them accountable.

You may be thinking to yourself, "My family will never follow a list!" If they won't, go on strike for a few days and see if they come around. You are not the hired help, you are family. Make sure your family knows how to treat you as such.

Our goal for you: If you don't already have one, write down a list of your goals, your bucket list, if you will. Then chunk it down into smaller pieces and engage the support of your family in achieving those goals—do not have them do what's on the list, but instead do other things that will free you up to realize your dreams. It is critically important for our sons and daughters to see us realizing our dreams, so they will have a role model to follow as they realize theirs.

Lessons Learned: Taking Care of You

Don't forget about you!

Using the Checklist: Taking Care of You

- ☐ Am I scheduling so I also have some down time?

- ☐ What have I done for me this month?

- ☐ Am I getting enough sleep and exercise?

- ☐ Do I have a list of dreams and wishes for myself?

- ☐ What am I going to do this month for myself?

- ☐ Does my family have the information they need to help me realize my dreams?

3.16 Being a Role Model

Keep in Mind: We're going to repeat our favorite James Baldwin quote again, just as we did in *Not All Kids Do Drugs*: "Children are not very good at listening to their elders, but they never fail to mimic them." If you can just keep in the back of your mind the thought that your children are always watching you, and that what they see you do is very close to what they will do as they live their lives, you will be a better parent and a better person. We are unbelievably powerful at influencing our children—let's make sure we respect that power and wield it carefully. Your children want to be just like you—make sure that's a good thing by modeling the values you hold dear.

Lessons Learned: Role Modeling

When it comes to our children, we are always on stage. Picture your children doing what you are doing right now—are you comfortable with that?

Using the Checklist: Role Modeling

☐ Am I being careful to be a good role model, especially when or if I use alcohol?

☐ What is the message I'm sending to my child today?

3.17 Remembering Intention

Keep In Mind: In the Tao, there is an amazingly powerful concept: Most people fail just when they are on the verge of success; so give as much care to the end as to the beginning and there will be no failure.

Think back to the beginning of your family, to the first day you became a parent—before all the work and the obligation and the exhaustion of parenting. What were your dreams on that day? How did you see the relationship you would have with your child? Do you remember the milestones—first word, first step—and the wild excitement they brought?

As our children grow older and more complicated, and our lives get busier and busier, it's easy to forget the passion we had for parenting. By the time our kids get to high school, it's tempting to think they are done with us, and sadly, we with them. This is not true!

As our children become teenagers and young adults, there is still so much to do; and they still dearly need our input. When the exhaustion, and possibly the disappointment start to creep in, try to go back in your mind to those first dreams, those first passions. The child you had so much love for you thought your heart would break is still there—they're just hiding inside that teenage disguise. If you can find a way to stay enthusiastic about being a parent, you will model the most important message of all—"You are everything to me"—and by doing so, you will create from your children parents with as much skill and passion as you have. Give as much care to the end as you did to the beginning—there is no greater gift you can give your family, or the world; and no better way to protect your children from the notion that drugs and alcohol are required for them to feel the way they want to feel.

Lessons Learned: Remember Your Intentions

Your baby is still your baby. You can raise your child in a way that allows you both to be your best selves, separately and together. It's all the little things you say and do that make it possible.

Using the Checklist: Intention

☐ Can I spend 5 minutes thinking about the excitement of my children today?

Part 4

Everything I Ever Learned About Parenting
I Learned at Disneyland

Obviously, the hyperbolic title of this section is an overstatement, but it captures the essence of what we want to communicate—parenting, both good and bad, can be very educational when you watch other people do it; and some of the most fascinating opportunities to watch the limitless varieties of parenting styles in action occur at the Disney parks. For many of the parents we see, a Disney visit is more about stress than it is about recreation, and we often wonder how much more fun these parents and their families would have on their visits if they were able to employ some of the Lessons Learned we've talked about in the first three sections of this handbook.

What we'll attempt to do in this section is apply some of those lessons to real life situations in an effort to applaud those going about it proactively, and gently nudge those parents who aren't quite there yet onto a different, more productive path. By reducing stress, stopping physical and emotional abuse, and building better relationships and communication styles with their families, these parents will be lessening the likelihood their children will end up using drugs and alcohol to change the way they feel.

Keep in Mind: *Kelly writes:* I have been a Disney junkie since the day I first set foot on Main Street in the Anaheim Park. As I walk toward the passageway which leads under the railroad tracks and into the park, I always make a point to look up at the quote from Walt that hangs there—"Here you leave today and enter the world of yesterday, tomorrow and fantasy." Every time I read that, I am swept away from my life of responsibility and the reality of my job, and I am transported to a place of comfort and relief.

On our first date, I told Jonathan that if we stayed friends, I'd take him to Disneyland one day. Of course, it turned out to be way more than that—we went to Walt Disney World for our honeymoon, and our daughter's first of her literally hundreds of visits to

Disneyland was the day she turned one. I don't think my love of all things Disney is only about the parks, though; I also admire the creativity, the positivity, and the stubborn refusal to accept failure as a final result that Walt Disney embodied throughout his entire life. While no human can be flawless, I admire Mr. Disney for the good things he stood for, and stood up for; and when you get right down to it, what kind of person, deep down, doesn't love the positive, proactive innocence of Mickey Mouse? *September 2011*

How to Use This Section

We're fully aware that everyone reading this handbook doesn't live 15 minutes away from a Disney park like we do, but this section is still perfectly applicable, even for people who find themselves less geographically blessed than we are. If you don't live close to Disneyland, simply substitute a public place you like to visit with your family for the purpose of recreation—beaches, public parks, lakes, baseball or soccer complexes, etc.

Instead of putting the Lessons Learned sections at the end, as we have in the preceding parts, here we are going to use them to open the sections for discussion. We will occasionally paraphrase or rewrite the lessons so they accurately reflect the issue being discussed. As you read, please reflect upon the parenting styles you observe others using when you are enjoying your favorite family outing spot, restaurant, or other public gathering place. Consider how these concepts apply to your family and how you might use them to build strong bonds and raise healthy, low stress kids.

As your children's primary role models, how you act and speak teaches your children the skills they will need in order to navigate their adolescent and teen years without using drugs and alcohol. It's not always clear how these topics affect drug and alcohol use, but we urge you to recall that drugs are less the problem and more the symptom of another problem which isn't being handled in a better way. In our opinion, these discussions represent the better way.

Lessons Learned: Reactive language

◆ Reactive language starts from a base of negativity.
◆ Reactive statements make the problem the focus of discussion.
◆ Reactive language creates an atmosphere of powerlessness, failure, and blame.

The Words We Use: Reactive language

Over the past year (2011), we've heard the following comments by parents about taking their children to Disneyland:

- *"I'd rather stick needles in my eyes than take my family to Disneyland!"*
- *"It is so stressful to take my family to Disneyland that I need a Xanax to walk through the gate."*
- *"I'm not going to waste my money taking my kids to Disneyland until they are old enough to understand it." (The children were eight years old at the time.)*

In the same year, we've heard the following from parents who were at Disneyland:

- *"Don't worry honey; it will only be dark and scary for a few minutes."*
- *"The pirates are going to get you!"*
- *"You won't like this ride, so just tough it out."*
- *"I sure hope this ride doesn't make you sick."*
- *"This ride looks stupid!"*
- *"Shows are a waste of our money and time. While we're at a park, I only want to ride the rides."*
- *"Be a man! This ride isn't that fast—don't be a baby!"*
- *"There's no way you are going to get me on that ride!"*
- *"It's not a real mountain! Grow up!"*
- *"That ride looks like it's going to break while we're on it."*
- *"You guys don't want to go on that ride, do you?"*

Parents who speak to their children or each other this way either create problems where none exist or make existing problems worse.

Lessons Learned: Proactive Language

◆ Positive proactive language makes for healthy communication and encourages responsibility. Seemingly small things when your kids are young become big things as they get older—patterns are powerful.
◆ You may have been deeply conditioned to be reactive, but you can change with awareness and effort.
◆ Perspective is everything. The same situation can be seen as controllable or controlling.
◆ Find another way to say it, and you can create a new way to do it!
◆ You model positive proactive language for your children. They will behave much the way you do.

The Words We Use: Proactive language

"When I walk through the gates of Disney, all my troubles melt away. It's a world of comfort where I get to spend time with my boys and enjoy my life. Disneyland is filled with warm childhood memories for me!" *--Michelle Gouvion, a mom and a friend*

Not everything we overhear at Disneyland is reactive. Some parents have mastered the power of proactive language and use it to create opportunities for their children to explore new experiences and savor familiar ones. In 2011, we also heard parents say:

◆ *"The fun part is that we get to hold hands in the dark for a couple of minutes."*
◆ *"The pirates are my favorite part of the ride—Yo Ho, Yo Ho—you're going to love them just like me!"*
◆ *"Let's rank our favorite rides at the end of the day."*
◆ *"What do you think about this ride?"*
◆ *"Let's alternate riding rides and seeing shows. Maybe some of us could do shows while the rest of us just do rides."*

- *"I think you'll like this ride better when you're two inches taller. That won't take long at all, the way you're growing!"*
- *"I think I'm going to skip this ride, but you guys go have fun!"*
- *"It's not a real mountain—this one is just for fun."*
- *"I hear that Disney has the best safety record."*
- *"I love it when I get to whisper in your ear in the dark."*

Lesson Learned: Reducing Fear; Increasing Confidence

One of the best parts of Disneyland is the conflict between good and evil. The villains can be some of the most powerful characters your children see when they visit, but it's easy for adults to forget that they can seem very real to young children.

How we handle the feelings the villains inspire in our children will either set them up for success or predispose them to failure. It breaks our hearts when we hear parents ridicule their children for being "babies" when they are afraid of the villains.

The Words We Use: The Power of, "Boo! Hiss!"

A lot of the fear children experience when they see a villain stems from their feelings of powerlessness over the evil character. You can give your children power over the bad guys by teaching them to chant, "Boo! Hiss!" when they come onscreen or onstage.

This simple phrase gives your children power over the situation—and lets them say to the villain, "I see you! You're not going to get away with your evil schemes!" They can do this for pirates, witches, spiders, and any other creepy characters they are confronted with. Obviously, you want to teach your children to do this in such a way as to not interfere with other audience members' opportunity to enjoy the show or movie; but you'll be surprised by the huge laugh the audience lets out when a three-year-old girl yells, "Boo! Hiss!" when Jafar comes onstage at the Aladdin show. You can also practice this at home whenever a bad guy comes onscreen.

Whatever else you can do to take away the power of the villain will help your children feel less fearful. We once got a good chuckle when we overheard a parent in a theater whisper to her child, "That evil witch should try wearing a new color to match her green skin!" Nobody experiencing real fear could giggle like the little girl did in response, and that's exactly the point.

Lessons Learned: Talking About Money

Children should understand that all the things the family has and receives cost money. Very young children won't have any sort of perspective on how much a lot or a little money is, but they should be familiar with the concept that the things we have don't just appear out of thin air. Talk with your children about how much it costs to go on vacation, to dine out, and to go to amusement parks. If you get your children involved in money management at an early age, they will gain respect for the work involved in attaining goals. Money issues, however, should not be used as a means to manipulate children or make them feel guilty for having basic needs or being a member of the family.

The Words We Use: Reactive Language

Another of our Disneyland 2011 reactive language champs was recently heard to utter:

"I spent a lot of money on this trip! We are going to have fun, or we're going home!"

Keep in Mind: Please don't lay a big guilt trip on your kids over the money you spent getting to and staying at your destination. Special trips and vacations cost money, but some parents we see are so worried they won't wring every penny of value out of every dollar they've spent that they force their children to carry on when they are tired, burned out, overheated, sunburned, thirsty and hungry. We've even seen parents ushering kids around the park who are so obviously ill that they have no business being out of bed. Money is important, but it's not so important that you need to endanger your children's health (and everyone who comes in contact with them) in an effort to get the most return on your investment.

It's a good idea to give your children a set sum of money they have to manage for the duration of your stay. This is a skill most children don't learn until they are older; and even then too

140

many of them learn by getting into deep financial difficulty and wasting weeks, months, or years digging their way back out. The lesson doesn't have to come with such a high personal price tag if we teach our young children budgeting and delayed gratification.

Lessons Learned: Chunk it Down to Reduce Stress

Almost anything will become unpleasant when done to excess. A back rub feels great, but if someone rubbed your back for 12 hours it would be the equivalent of physical torture. Set limits on how much time you are going to commit to a particular activity if you want to keep things pleasant, reduce stress, and teach your children patience and forethought.

Keep in Mind: There is nothing quite as dramatic as the Disney meltdown. Too many times we've seen over-stimulated, exhausted, stressed out children reach their breaking point and perform their own version of the China Syndrome. The question this begs is: Which part of this is the fun part? This is not the fault of the children—the parents have dropped the ball in the time management and scheduling departments. The secret is to plan your day in shorter segments; and to clearly communicate to your children how the day is going to go. If you outline what you will be doing and when you will be doing it before you head out, your children will know what to expect.

Hopefully, by now, you have learned that such thoughts as, "There is no way my kid is going to leave Disneyland after three hours without losing it!" are reactive and defeatist in nature. We have close friends and neighbors who repeatedly tell us, "I could never take my kids to Disneyland for a few hours. It's not worth the fight trying to get them out of the park." Unfortunately, by choosing to stay reactive, they are robbing themselves of hours of pleasure and valuable time spent with their children.

There are two issues at play here. First, the children are putting up a stink because they want something: to stay longer at the park. They continue to put up that stink every time because it worked before and it continues to work for them now. They can't comprehend that by behaving the way they do, they eliminate the likelihood of future visits occurring any time soon. Second, the parents have failed to make the costs of the children's actions clear to them, and they have also failed to show how cooperation now means continued benefits being realized in the future.

To make the short term visits work, you need to plan ahead and set boundaries before you go. Maybe you could lay out a plan like this:

- *"On Monday, we'll go from eight in the morning until 10:30. We can do stuff in Adventureland, but then mommy has to come home and work."*
- *"On Friday, we'll go over at four in the afternoon, ride all the rides in Tomorrowland; then we'll watch the dancing for a while and catch the fireworks show from the top of the parking garage on our way out."*
- *"Next week, we'll do two mornings in California Adventure. You can look at the map and choose which areas you'd like to visit."*

When 10:30 Monday morning rolls around and it's time to leave, if your children start to whine and pitch a fit, calmly explain to them that whining now will have repercussions on the plans you have for Friday. If you have laid the groundwork we talked about before in the yelling section, your children will understand that you mean what you say and that they have a choice here—follow the plan and reap the benefits, or mess around and lose the very thing they want so much right now: more time in the park. You have to keep up your end of the bargain if you want this to work, though. If you promise to take them on a certain day, they need to have confidence you will keep your word. If you don't, why should they play by your rules any more?

You'll also benefit by maximizing what you get done with the time you have allotted. Some days, all we do is see shows. Other days, we will dedicate all our time to a particular area or land in the park. Some days we won't do any of the standard stuff—we might just wander the parks looking for hidden Mickeys (Google it!) and watching people. Don't waste the valuable time you have by chasing rides all over the park and spending most of your day trying to weave your way through the crowds. If you are on a trip where you're staying in a hotel, plan for times when you can go back, sit around the pool and decompress by reading quietly or playing in the water. The "No Whining" rule should always be in place, though. If your child wants to spend time whining, it should come with a consequence.

Lessons Learned: Reduce Your Stress by Quieting Your Mind

If you look, you can find quiet places anywhere you go. There are entire websites, blogs and podcasts dedicated to helping you find quiet hideaways at Disneyland and Walt Disney World. When our daughter was little, we would go to them during naptime and enjoy the park's quiet little moments with a good paperback or audio book. Here's a list of our favorite spots. Get in touch with us if you have some favorites, and we'll include them in future publications.

Establish a Pattern: Places to Relax at Disneyland

- The area where the quartet with antique instruments plays in the back alleyway of New Orleans Square between the bathroom by the railroad and the Blue Bayou restaurant. They are fantastic, and completely relaxing.
- There is a three-piece jazz band that plays in the French Market Restaurant. You can get a mint julep and some Mickey-shaped beignets while you sit and relax.
- The downstairs deck at the Hungry Bear Restaurant is quiet and has great bathrooms. Bring your lunch, or order food upstairs. We have a tradition of saving all of our bread crusts, sometimes for weeks, so we can feed the ducks there while watching the boats and canoes. It's a wonderful, cool, quiet place to take a break.
- The bridge by the pond next to Thunder Mountain. Don't go too close to the smokers; they tend to wander away from their designated spot for smoking. (Rule breakers!)
- The Grand Californian Hotel: inside on any couch on the first or third floors, or in front of the fireplace. Bring a book (Kindles, Nooks, and iPads work too) and read while your child takes a nap in the stroller.

- There are many places in California Adventure to stop and relax, but the Pacific Wharf Café has a little side area next to the water where you can see the parades and take a cool break.
- Find your own quiet place, and make it a point to take a break to people watch. You don't have to go full force.
- The animation class in California Adventure is one of our all-time favorites. It is a comfortable, relaxing, air conditioned way to pass 20 minutes. We will sometimes do it three or four times in a row. Save the characters you draw, no matter how bad you think they are. We have a blast looking back at some of our past efforts—and we actually have improved over the years!

Lesson Learned: Organize Your Trip; Reduce Your Frustration

Since the advent of the Internet, failure to plan ahead is a conscious choice. If you are the type that values spontaneity, great—as long as you can roll with all the punches that come with it. A lot of the people we see who profess belief in spontaneity are actually just bad at planning ahead, and they prove it by going ballistic when the frustration and confusion caused by their bad planning overwhelm them.

Keep in Mind: Planning and organizing with websites and maps will reduce your frustration as it teaches your family valuable skills. As you enter the park, pick up a map and schedule for everyone—not just mom or dad. Letting your kids learn how to read the Disneyland map (or any park map) is a great way to learn mapping skills, plot and plan courses, practice reading, take measurements, and learn compass points. Yes, your iPhone has an app for that, but you should still teach your children how to read a map. A map will still get you out of the San Bernardino National Forest after you drop it on a rock; your iPhone, not so much.

When you plan your route through the park with a map, it's fun to look back at where you've been and to plan where you'll go next by circling and numbering the locations. Turn your map into a list and rank your favorites. Let your kids read about the park rules, emergency information and special places listed on the map. Use a map to plan your next visit, make lists of things you want to do, and set goals for when and how you can return in the near future. Write the date of your visit on your map and put it in your scrapbook.

If you're going to an unfamiliar Disney location, take the time to visit some of the blogs or chat forums before you go. There is enough insider information out there to fill the Library of Congress. Just a little advice from people who know what they're talking about is very effective for keeping your stress level down as you try to navigate unfamiliar territory.

Lesson Learned: Teaching Manners

Good manners lead to self-confidence, and self-confidence reduces potential drug abuse. Kindness lasts a lifetime.

Keep In Mind: When you dine outside your home, you will almost always do so at a restaurant or party. Good manners will serve you and your children very well in both places. Polite, well-behaved children will get you better service at restaurants. Tired, overworked servers will avoid you like the plague if your children are behaving like shaved monkeys.

Even if your children are really fast eaters, teach them to stay at the table until others are finished eating. Our experience is that once the first kid is up and gone, the rest want to get up and go join in the fun. The children who didn't finish eating in their rush to go play will be the same ones having the hunger meltdown two hours later—usually just as the fireworks or Fantasmic are starting.

Keep in Mind: Good manners require that if you make a mess, you should clean it up. Disney parks are famous for being immaculate, but the staff isn't there to be your servants. We understand that babies have no understanding that the Cheerios they are raining down on the carpet will have to be cleaned up by someone, but if you leave an area in such a state that the staff can't decide if they should vacuum or shovel, you are not using good manners. If your children have strewn crayons, napkins and placemats over half the restaurant, have them clean up after themselves before you depart. It is an act of simple respect for others, and it teaches your children responsibility and good manners.

Keep In Mind: Backpacks are a great way to transport large amounts of stuff around the park without having to have your hands full, but good manners include being aware of how much space your backpack is filling. When you pivot in place while wearing your backpack, you can put your children, other people's children, and short adults like Kelly on the ground without even realizing it. Be aware of your space. On the same note, light sabers and pirate swords are great fun, but not when wielded with indiscriminate abandon by a four year old in a crowd. America's Funniest Home Videos doesn't need any more clips of people getting whacked in spots they'd rather not be whacked in.

Keep in Mind: Good manners mean you don't pick flowers in public places. We've actually heard parents defending their kid's flower picking by saying, "It's only one flower. What's the harm?" There are 50,000 people in the park! If they all pick just one, the place will look like a plague of locusts descended. Also, standing in the flowerbeds to get a better view of the parade is thoughtless and rude. Don't teach your children to get what they want at the expense of the greater good.

The Words We Use: Don't Abuse the Characters; Preserve the Magic

- We've heard parents tell a child, "Johnny, go kick Tigger." In what world is it OK to tell your child to kick someone? Kelly is seriously non-violent, but this tests that limit.
- Please don't ruin the magic of the characters by saying things like, "Wow! That girl was great at playing Snow White!" You have to remember, the four-year-old behind you in line thinks that girl IS Snow White. We all have to spend a lot of years knowing the truth—there's no need to rush it for the little ones.
- That line standing patiently with their cameras and autograph books has been there for a while. Please don't tell your children to "just jump in there and I'll get a quick photo." It's just not polite.

Lessons Learned: Education is Everywhere

Disneyland is famous for their lines. Waiting in line doesn't have to be an exercise in bored shuffling of feet. Memory is enhanced when it is coupled up with a sensory experience, and the wide variety of environments created by the Disney Imagineers provides great opportunities for learning, practicing, and memorizing. Learning doesn't just happen at desks—all those amazing kids you see in the national spelling bees are famous for learning in different venues.

Keep in Mind: You can memorize poems, learn geography, practice spelling words, and go over math facts while in line at Disneyland. We've practiced spelling words by making up sentences on the Haunted Mansion ride—every sentence had to have Jack Skellington and the spelling word in it. Our daughter howled with laughter the whole time, and she got 100% of the words right on the test. We do math by adding receipts, figuring out gratuities, and counting things like characters in parades. We have also practiced geography while riding through Small World. All of Disneyland, or wherever you go, can be used as a classroom.

Youth Enrichment Programs

People who homeschool their children know something that few others do—the YES (Youth Enrichment Series) programs at both Disney parks (California and Florida) are fantastic. They offer classes ranging from science, physics, leadership and art to history, animation, music and performing arts. These are educational and competitive programs.

Another fun way to learn with Disney is The Kingdom Keepers Quest, which is based on a book series that involves problem solving, visualization, observation, creativity, math skills, language arts and critical thinking. We encourage all parents to review this educational series. If you are a pass holder, the additional cost is very reasonable. http://www.disneyyouth.com/

The Kim Possible World Showcase Adventure at Epcot is another way that kids can learn geography and history while learning to defeat bad guys using information from the different country pavilions at Walt Disney World.

http://disneyworld.disney.go.com/parks/epcot/attractions/kim-possible/

Lesson Learned: Teach Your Children Respect for Other Nationalities

Teaching your children respect for people from other walks of life will allow them to appreciate the differences and embrace the similarities found in all nationalities. It will also increase their knowledge of geography and history while it enhances their skills at interacting with other children and adults.

Keep in Mind: A major amusement venue like Disneyland is a terrific place to observe different languages and customs. When we hear people speaking a different language, we talk about how it sounds to us and try to see if we can figure out what the words mean if we listen closely. We often will stop and talk to families visiting from other places, and we try to welcome them to our wonderful state and offer help if it is their first visit to Disneyland.

Every cast member (Disney employee) wears a nametag with their home city and state or their home country on it, just under their name. Reading nametags is a great way to meet people from all over the world, especially when you visit Epcot at Walt Disney World. It is not rude to ask a cast member about their home country; it is encouraged. Stop for a minute, and let them tell your children about their language and the beauty of their homeland.

Lesson Learned: Look for Teachable Moments—Don't Just Ride the Rides

Live theater, musical performances, dancing, and role playing are huge parts of the Disney experience. Live shows are a great way to teach an appreciation for the arts while also teaching your children how to be polite audience members. Being a good audience member is something your children should practice from the time they are small, as it teaches them to respect not only the cast but also the other members of the audience.

Keep in Mind: When you get a chance, talk to the performers. At Disney parks, children can see up close how an instrument is played or how a dance step is executed. We've had opportunities to learn dance moves, get detailed information about antique musical instruments, learn how to play a fiddle, and speak with a blues musician who worked at the park way back when Walt was still in charge.

Theater Manners

Public arts venues are great places to practice good manners, and Disneyland is packed with them. The great thing about Disneyland is that everyone understands that a large part of any audience is going to be children, so staff and audience members expect that kids will make mistakes. Better they learn theater skills at the park than to have a major embarrassment when you try to take your children to a much more formal venue.

Whether we are seeing a barbershop quartet, a marching band, or a dramatic performance, we try to practice good theater manners. We try to make eye contact with the performers, and to smile if it is appropriate—you don't want to be grinning like a loon when Simba's father dies. If Q&A sessions are offered, we practice asking questions about the performance, or the costumes, so we can learn something new each time we see a performance.

As a role model, you should try to practice good manners so your children can learn from you. If you have a cell phone, turn it off when you are in a show. Texting while the show is going on is a distraction to others around you, and it is rude—even if you think it's OK because you're "not making any noise." The spotlight glow of your screen is distraction enough, and that makes it bad manners to use it. If you can just watch the show, you can also model for your children the art of being in the moment, a very important life skill.

Also, if you have a very young child who is in a meltdown, take them out of the theater. Disney has provisions for you to exit safely, and cast members will make sure you can find your way. There is no reason you should teach your children that it's OK to ruin the show for everyone else by staying in the theater as you tend to your screaming child. The show just isn't that important, and there's another one in 20 minutes anyway—come back then.

Teacher Tip

One of our schools has a class that teaches students how to listen to speakers, how to ask questions, when to applauded, how long to applaud, and when you should stand up during applause breaks. You can do the same while you reap the additional benefits of breaking up the heat and exhaustion of the day by spending a few minutes enjoying an air-conditioned show.

Keep in Mind:
- You can teach your children to be keen observers by looking for hidden Mickeys. There are books and websites dedicated to the fine art of searching for the Mickey ears hidden in patterns all over the parks and hotels. It's like being a detective searching for clues, and it will keep your kids entertained as you walk and wait, two things you may find yourself doing a lot of. Teach your kids that waiting doesn't have to be torture, if you plan ahead and use your imagination.
- Learn the stories behind the names painted in the windows all over the Disney parks. Each name represents an individual who played a pivotal role in the development or expansion of some aspect of the Disney experience.
- Making smashed pennies is a great way to create a memory of each visit. There are so many smashed penny machines in the Disney parks, however, that you have to prioritize if you don't want to go bankrupt. This is a great opportunity to practice observation skills—some machines are tucked away in hidden corners—and also a great way to practice delayed gratification. It's also a fun collection to take to show and tell.

Lesson Learned: Delayed Gratification

Children with the skill to delay gratification will be happier, healthier young adults with a lower potential to use drugs and alcohol.

Keep In Mind: Buy balloons at the end of the day. Balloons can become a parent's worst enemy in a crowd, even though they can make it easier to find your stroller after a ride. If you teach a young child to make a plan and get a balloon at the end of the day instead of the minute you walk through the gates, you can teach them delayed gratification at a young age. If they start crying, show them the money and tell them they get to be in charge of buying the perfect balloon as the evening winds down. Otherwise, all day long, you will be bobbing and weaving through the crowd with your balloon bonking you and everyone else in the head as you do. Also, if you wait until later in the day to get a balloon, you can lessen the chance your kid will find a way to untie the string and send it drifting away to balloon heaven while they scream bloody murder in panic and frustration.

Lessons Learned: Family Goal Setting and the Annual Pass

Setting goals is an important life skill. Making an annual pass a family goal is a way to teach that skill while working toward something fun and educational.

Keep In Mind: An annual pass to an amusement park is a great way for your teen to enjoy the company of their friends while in a safe environment. We can't speak for other parks, but Disneyland has so much security, both in uniform and out, that it would be hard for your kids to get away with anything, including the use of drugs and alcohol, while on a Disney property. Your kids get a chance to feel a little grown up when they go off on their own for a while, but make sure they check back in with you in person frequently. They should not have free run of the park for extended periods, since unsupervised teenagers in a group are a recipe for disaster even Disney security can't control perfectly.

Dancing
There are several places to dance at Disneyland. Our favorite is the Plaza Gardens, where a swing band plays every Friday and Saturday night. There are couples who started dancing there in 1955 when it opened who are still there, dancing like the kids they were, to this day. Even now, the dance floor is filled with incredibly talented

young dancers who are more than willing to show an interested child a few moves and encourage that child's interest with heartfelt enthusiasm. What great role models they are for younger kids watching from the sidelines! As we watch the men in Zoot suits and the women in multi-layered petticoats whirling and jumping, it's like being in a scene from a movie. We'll often spend an entire evening listening to music, watching the dancers, and chatting with the couples playing canasta who have been playing cards at the same tables for many decades. Our daughter fills her backpack with games, books, and art supplies and has a fantastic time switching from activity to activity all night long. What a great goal for a family to work toward!

Disney Endurance Series: Goal Setting and Exercise

Disney has an endurance series for runners and walkers. It consists of fun runs, 5K's, and a series half and full marathons. They are a little expensive, but they are great, well-organized, fantasy-filled runs. Not only do you get to go backstage during the runs, but all the characters are also out waving to you and posing for pictures along the way. It is a great goal for a single member or an entire family to commit to, and you can either train together or support the person participating as they train.
http://espnwwos.disney.go.com/sports/rundisney/

Moms' Exercise Club
Kelly has an entire route laid out through the parks and hotels, which can be used for jogging or speed walking. After dropping the kids off at school, a group will meet for exercise and be back in the office by mid-morning. It's your annual pass too, mom—do something just for you once in a while.

Lessons Learned: Teach Your Children Respect for Their Bodies by Protecting Them

When children learn to respect their health and their bodies, they are less likely to use drugs and alcohol.

Keep in Mind: When you go to Disneyland or any other amusement park, one thing you can count on is that you are going to be doing a boatload of walking. In this case, fashion is not your friend. It's not that you can't look good and be functional at the same time, but you cannot decide what shoes to wear at Disneyland based solely on what they look like. Yes, those five-inch wedge heels accent your toned calves, but the bloody blisters you'll have by the end of the day can detract from that look. We can't count the number of young women (and grown women, for that matter) we've seen tottering through the park in heels that are clearly uncomfortable and, in some cases, just downright dangerous. Be kind to your feet.

Your children are probably not very good at shoe selection when they are young. If your daughter insists on wearing her princess shoes to the park, pack a set of athletic shoes or Crocs for when she realizes what a bad decision that was.

Parents need to be sensitive to their children's experience as well as their own. Kelly recently saw a couple running the Disneyland 5K with their son, who couldn't have been more than six. The adults were decked out in the finest high-end running garb, including the best-of-the-best shoes. Their son, however, had on surf shoes with no socks and was wearing a heavy sweater on a day when a light tee shirt was appropriate. He was in agony. He wailed and cried the entire time, and his oblivious parents couldn't understand what the matter was. They just kept yelling at him to hurry up, and berating him for ruining their experience. Sometimes we think there should be a test you have to pass before you are allowed to become parents.

Keep in Mind: Protect your skin with sunscreen and hats; and hydrate, hydrate, hydrate. You might not need detailed instructions on how to apply sunscreen, but we see people who get fooled by a few simple things when they visit California from elsewhere. We are blessed with really low humidity most of the year, and people who are used to sweating profusely in humid climates don't realize they are sweating just as much here, it's just drying really fast. We see families dropping like flies from heat stroke and dehydration all year, so an ounce of prevention will go a long way here. Also, don't forget to put sunscreen on the tops of your children's feet if they are wearing open shoes. It's not pretty to see ravaged, burned feet caused by this oversight.

Keep in Mind: Protect your stomachs. Yes, it's an amusement park, but try to limit the salt, fat, sugar, and caffeine. It's true—nobody has ever vomited at Disneyland. That doesn't mean no one has ever emptied the contents of their stomach into the street, it's just that, at Disneyland, this is referred to as a "protein spill." Try to teach your children to eat small quantities frequently, and to intersperse the junk with a few healthy snacks and some fruit during the day. It's a lesson that will serve them well at school, college, and work as they grow older.

Lessons Learned: Reduce Your Stress; Reduce Your Children's Stress

Patience under trying circumstances is a teachable skill. Try to model it for your children. By being in tune with your children and their needs, you can make everyone's day more enjoyable.

Keep in Mind: Children cry when they are overwhelmed. Expect that it will happen, and try to figure out what the reason for it is. The list is pretty basic: injured, tired, hungry, hot, cold, frustrated, over-stimulated, and need a potty. It will not help to scream at them to be quiet—that is not a solution to any of the above conditions.

Strollers
It's a fine line between the right time to use a stroller and when a stroller deprives your child an opportunity to struggle a little. Make sure you have a stroller for a child who needs it—a day at the park can entail walking for miles, and little bodies work a lot harder to cover a mile than big bodies do. At the same time, walking is good for your children. Wean them off the stroller over a number of visits, and talk to them about the timetable for doing so. If your kid can go on Indiana Jones, they can walk (you have to be really tall to ride Indiana Jones).

Side-by-Side Strollers

If you have twins, side-by-side strollers are great. Side-by-side strollers are not great at amusement parks, however. They don't fit anywhere, and you are going to stress yourself unnecessarily if you try to navigate the park in the stroller equivalent of a Hummer.

The Baby Center

Like most amusement parks, Disneyland has a baby center. It is the quietest, nicest, cleanest, coolest place in the park. When you step in the door, a cast member dressed like a nanny will greet you, and, as the cool air hits you, you'll marvel at how quiet it is. It's like being inside a world insulated by a huge cotton ball, and it's wonderful. There are books for kids, teeny little chairs, and the cutest little potties designed just for toddlers. Your kids will love it, you'll love it, and your stress hormones will get a 15-minute break as well.

The Baby Switchback Pass

You don't have to build up a huge well of resentment toward your child because they are keeping you off of your favorite ride due to the fact they don't meet the height requirements. Split up. One parent can go on the ride first, and there is often a singles line that moves really fast. When you get off, ask any cast member for a switchback pass, and they will gladly hand you a card that allows your significant other instant access to the Speedpass line. It's great, it saves time, and it allows you to have fun too.

Lesson Learned: Yelling and Hitting Increase Stress

For most psychologists and professionals who work with children, yelling and hitting have been relegated to the dustbin of bad methods for building healthy, emotionally sound children. Unfortunately, they are both behaviors many parents have historically employed, and they continue to perpetuate as the children who are hit and yelled at carry that legacy forward by doing the same to their kids. When you are at an amusement park, it is not OK to spank your children at any time, but it's especially not OK to hit them or scream at them because they are afraid to go on a ride.

155

Kelly writes: The first time my daughter ever heard me yell was at a stranger on the Thunder Mountain rollercoaster. A dad was trying to force a hysterical three-year-old to go on a ride she was obviously terrified of. As she wailed at the top of her lungs and struggled desperately to escape, the cast members in charge of the ride were smart enough to not send the coaster. I was so disturbed that this father would willingly traumatize his child for the sake of a silly rollercoaster ride that I confronted him and demanded that he take his child off the ride. Not only was this dad emotionally abusing his child, he was doing the same to every other child on the ride as well. My daughter's eyes were the size of saucers, and she was obviously horrified a parent would do such a thing to a child. Finally, this ape relented and took his daughter off the ride.

Unfortunately, it did not end there. As we were exiting the ride, my daughter and I were stunned to see this father spanking his child and yelling at her about how she had ruined everything. I immediately instructed a cast member to call security, and went to confront the man again. Luckily, security arrived, but it was extremely upsetting for everyone who witnessed this nightmare of bad parenting run amok. I have never forgotten this man, and I worry about his child. There is no way she is not being traumatized by that parent and his inability to deal with his own feelings; and there is no way his physical and emotional abuse is not turning her into a child more likely to deal with her emotions in a dysfunctional way. There are last chance exits on every ride at Disneyland, and I never fail to point them out to parents having a difficult time with a scared child. *September 2011*

Lesson Learned: Reduce Fear by Turning a Negative Into a Positive

Some children are going to be afraid of rides—that's just the way it is. That doesn't mean we have to scream at them and hit them, however. Sometimes, healthy peer pressure can help your children overcome the fear they may have about going on a ride or doing something scary. If you can arrange for another kid to sit with the scared child and speak encouraging words, it might help overcome the fear. When a younger child sees an older sibling doing

156

something fun and a little scary, it might be the perfect motivation to get them on the ride as well.

Our daughter has been scared of a couple of rides for quite a while. As we were writing this book, though, she had the chance to go on Splash Mountain with a good friend who is absolutely fearless. This friend encouraged our daughter to throw her hands high in the air on the final drop which leads to the big splash at the bottom, something she had been very reluctant to do up to that point. At the urging of her friend though, she threw caution to the wind and raised her hands high over her head as the ride hurtled toward the water. She was so thrilled and proud of herself when she got off the ride! The positive encouragement, a form of peer pressure, helped her overcome a fear and achieve a goal. It was very cool.

You can also desensitize your children to the experience of a scary ride by previewing the ride on YouTube. It would be hard to find a ride that doesn't have a video of it online. If you view these videos with your children, they can get used to the twists and turns before they experience it in real life. This has helped our daughter immensely in her efforts to ride Space Mountain, which she now considers to be one of her favorite rides. It was not always so.

Lessons Learned: Teaching Your Children to Respect Boundaries and Rules

Rules typically exist to protect the greater good. Littering is destructive and ugly, so there is a rule against it. Cigarette smoke is offensive, unhealthy, and deadly, so we have rules to limit the exposure of the non-smoking public to it. Most smokers are very aware of how they are perceived these days, and they try very hard to stay within the confines of the designated smoking areas assigned to them. A few, however, are so desperate to light up, or so disrespectful of the rules, that they feel the freedom to smoke where they please. We use these people as opportunities to talk to our daughter and her friends about how bad smoking is for human bodies, and about respecting rules and the rights of others.

Jonathan, as a former smoker, is a little more forgiving when it comes to smokers so desperate to light up that they do so before they have reached the smoking area, but Kelly is a bit of a noodge when it comes to smokers. She has very little tolerance for smoke, and doesn't take at all well to smokers who crush their butts on the ground when there is an ashtray provided for that purpose just a few feet away.

Conclusion

"We keep moving forward, opening new doors, and doing new things, because we're curious and curiosity keeps leading us down new paths." --Walt Disney.

The recurring themes discussed in this book are pride in oneself, establishing patterns, proactive language, organization, respect, manners, goal setting, consistency, stress reduction, confidence, communication, relationships, family—well, you get the point. There are a lot of themes in this book.

We want to point out one last time, though, how few of them have any direct connection to drug and alcohol use. The topics we discussed pertain more to the act of living a life that has a lower potential for drug and alcohol use simply because they are never seen as attractive or necessary.

Please take this checklist, and start checking things off. Don't do all of them by yourself, have your family play their parts as well. If you do, you are going to find you have a lot more time, and a lot more desire, to whisper sweet, positive, proactive things in your children's ears; and call other parents when there is a party; and stop being reactive; and explore your family values; and laugh and love and live with your family!

This is why we made the checklist. Now go use it!

The Mother's Checklist

Using the Checklist: When Should We Start Talking About Drugs?

☐ Have I started the conversation/Am I continuing the conversation?

☐ Do I appreciate my children's level of exposure to and awareness about drugs and alcohol?

☐ Am I checking to see if I understand what my child is actually asking?

☐ Am I educating myself a little each day?

☐ Am I misleading my children in the pursuit of comfort?

☐ Am I teaching my children about labels and dosages?

☐ Am I careful with my language concerning medicine?

☐ Did I discuss anti-drug ads that we may have seen together or can I arrange to find one to discuss?

☐ Did I find an opportunity to discuss a movie or TV show with drug or alcohol references in it?

☐ Did I find a negative example of public drug use and ask my child's opinion?

☐ Did I find at least one time to talk about a healthy lifestyle for our family?

Using the Checklist: Why Do Kids Use Drugs?

☐ Are my children stressed by over scheduling? What are my options if they are?

☐ Am I aware of the many forces that can cause stress in my children's lives?

☐ Do I have an accurate picture of who my children are and what their strengths and weaknesses are?

☐ Am I aware of the many forces that can cause stress in my children's lives?

☐ Do I have a plan that focuses on my children's strengths and helps them where they are struggling?

☐ Do my children have the social skills and self-confidence required for success?

☐ Are my children struggling to fit in? Are they making unhealthy decisions in order to be popular?

☐ Do my children have some down time?

☐ Is everyone getting enough sleep? How can I improve this situation if they aren't?

☐ Is my child a follower or a leader?

☐ Am I making time in my busy life to pay enough attention to my child?

Using the Checklist: How High Do You Float When You Get High?

☐ Am I conscious of the confusion drug and alcohol discussions can cause, both for me and my children?

☐ Do I know the difference between awareness and understanding?

- [ ] Do I check for understanding when I speak with my children? (Reiterate what the speaker has said to be sure both parties are on the same page.)
- [ ] Do I know that there is no tobacco in Tabasco?
- [ ] Have I tried to educate myself about drugs and alcohol recently?

Using the Checklist: Positive Proactive Language
- [ ] Do I recognize positive proactive speech when I speak it or hear it?
- [ ] Can I identify patterns of communication that I already have, and group them into positive and negative language? Am I more positive and proactive, or am I more reactive?
- [ ] Am I using positive and proactive language with myself?
- [ ] Am I doing the same with my spouse, others, and especially my children?
- [ ] Am I mindful of the way my words are interpreted by others?
- [ ] Am I setting an example of success with the language I use with my children?

Using the Checklist: Negative Reactive Language
- [ ] Am I monitoring my speech and eliminating negative and reactive language?
- [ ] Am I careful about using absolutes, like "all," "never," and "always?"
- [ ] Am I sensitive to absolute statements like, "All kids are going to drink eventually," and the chance that they will become self-fulfilling prophesies?
- [ ] Am I recognizing negative and reactive language in my thoughts?
- [ ] Am I recognizing it in others?
- [ ] Are my reactions overblown or exaggerated?
- [ ] Am I trying to stop pessimistic thinking and language?
- [ ] Am I being careful about labeling my children?
- [ ] Am I responding to my children, or am I reacting to them?

Using the Checklist: Problem Solving
- [ ] Am I verbalizing **identify, try/apply, resolve** problem solving techniques with my children regularly?
- [ ] Am I engaging my children in problem solving efforts regularly?

Using the Checklist: Patterns of Repetition
- [ ] Have I created a repetitive dialogue framework to use when my child is hurt or upset?
- [ ] Am I remembering to employ my key phrases when necessary?
- [ ] Am I really listening when my children tell me why they are crying?

Using the Checklist: Struggle
- [ ] Am I allowing my children the opportunity to struggle?

- [ ] Do I encourage my children to try again when their first attempt isn't successful?

- ☐ Have I modeled graceful failure/lessons learned/trying again recently?
- ☐ Have I shown my children how to use a pro/con list?
- ☐ Am I sensitive to the level of frustration my children can manage before they melt down? What can I do to increase their coping skills?

Using the Checklist: Self-Talk

- ☐ What is the tone of my inner speech? Am I mostly positive, or mostly negative?
- ☐ Am I recognizing and eliminating my own negative self-talk?
- ☐ Am I helping my children build positive "I am's"?
- ☐ Do I need some positive "I am's" of my own?
- ☐ Am I sensitive to the media images my child is exposed to?
- ☐ Does part of my negative self-talk include thoughts the positive proactive speech is just a bunch of hooey?
- ☐ Am I giving my children specific words to use in situations that cause them discomfort or distress?
- ☐ Am I helping my children to eliminate negative self-talk?
- ☐ Is there any chance that I secretly agree with the kids doing the teasing? Am I letting my children be who they are, or do I want them to be what I think they should be?

Using the Checklist: They Can Hear You

- ☐ Am I using referential speech and gossiping to give my children positive insights into how I see them?
- ☐ Am I careful to not be overheard when discussing something negative about my child that concerns me?
- ☐ Have I inadvertently labeled my children in a negative way?
- ☐ Is there any way nicknames that refer to my children might be hurting them?
- ☐ Am I careful to keep teasing at an absolute minimum, and eliminate it entirely if it has the power to hurt my children's feelings?
- ☐ Am I watching how I speak in front of my children?

Using the Checklist: Let's Work Together

- ☐ Are the adults in our family striving to present a unified front when discussing issues of health, safety, and family values?

Using the Checklist: The Drug Talk

- ☐ Am I talking to my children about drugs and alcohol on a regular basis?
- ☐ Have I told my children how I feel about this subject?
- ☐ Have I found a way to incorporate the topic of the other side of the user?

- ☐ Am I being careful about the stories my children hear about drug use?
- ☐ Do I have positive role models to discuss?

Using the Checklist: Listening

- [ ] What kind of listener am I?
- [ ] How might I best improve my listening skills?
- [ ] Am I practicing reflective listening?
- [ ] Am I listening to what my kids have to say?
- [ ] Am I encouraging my kids to talk, or am I cutting them off when I become frustrated?
- [ ] Am I trying to seek first to understand, and then to be understood?

Using the Checklist: Talking About Money

- [ ] Am I letting my kids add up purchases on the calculator?
- [ ] Am I talking about how much managing a household costs?
- [ ] Am I talking about how to save, earn, and budget?
- [ ] Am I conscious of the "Costco Effect," and actively trying to avoid impulse buying?
- [ ] Am I talking to my children about the consequences of poor money management?

Using the Checklist: Talking About Movies

- [ ] Am I using movies and other media to start conversations with my children?
- [ ] Am I using overly technical language before my children understand the basic concepts?

Using the Checklist: Medicine Cabinets, OTC Drugs

- [ ] Have I checked my "potential to kill my children drug overdose, addiction, and death locker" for expired drugs and drugs with the potential for abuse?
- [ ] Have I put abusable, dangerous, and addictive drugs in my home in a secure, monitored location?
- [ ] Am I being specific about the way I discuss medicine around my children?
- [ ] Am I reading my labels?
- [ ] Am I teaching my children about labels, dose information and warnings?
- [ ] Am I treating drugs the way they would be treated at a pharmacy?
- [ ] Do I have a system to give distasteful medicine to my kids?

Using the Checklist: Self-Medicating

- [ ] Am I being careful about self-prescribing and self-medicating?
- [ ] Do I have a clear picture of how much caffeine my children are consuming?
- [ ] Have I discussed the safe, supervised use of medications in our home?
- [ ] Do my children need my permission before they consume beverages that contain high levels of caffeine—energy drinks, brewed coffee, etc.?
- [ ] Am I closely monitoring the use of medications in my home, both pharmaceutical and OTC?

Using the Checklist: Yes and No Talk

- ☐ Am I saying no when I could have said yes?
- ☐ When I say no, am I offering alternative ideas?
- ☐ Do I find myself saying yes just to avoid being unpopular or to head off a fight?
- ☐ Do I say no when necessary, when issues of health and safety are on the line?

Using the Checklist: Conflict Resolution

- ☐ Am I helping my children learn how to deal with conflict?
- ☐ Am I listening to the problem while not letting accusations run wild?
- ☐ Am I making suggestions to help them without giving them the answers?
- ☐ Am I teaching my children to empathize with others who may be struggling with emotional difficulties?
- ☐ Am I teaching my child to socially engage other kids and adults?

Using the Checklist: Parenting Styles

- ☐ What is my predominant parenting style? Am I happy with what I find?
- ☐ Did I unintentionally adopt my parenting style from my parents? If so, am I OK with that?
- ☐ Are there any changes I could make that might put me more in line with the parent I want to be?
- ☐ Does my partner have the same style? If not, what can we do to make our styles more unified?

Using the Checklist: Boundaries

- ☐ Am I setting boundaries, or letting my kids run all over me?
- ☐ Am I being consistent in my words, actions, and boundaries?
- ☐ Is everyone who oversees my children part of a united front?
- ☐ Am I sensitive to the idea that the details of the rules will change as my children grow older, but that the core values must remain consistent?
- ☐ Do our family rules travel with us?

Using the Checklist: Manners

- ☐ Am I setting a good example by using good manners?
- ☐ Am I encouraging and teaching my children to use good manners, and gently correcting failures to do so?
- ☐ Am I role modeling and teaching kindness to my children?

Using the Checklist: Organizing

- ☐ Do I know where my checklist is? *Yes! It's in your hand! Check it off!*
- ☐ Have I identified what my children need to do, when they need to do it, and put it into a checklist they can use to be responsible for their own lives?
- ☐ Have I addressed the issue of clutter in my life?

- [ ] Do I have a monthly calendar set up?
- [ ] Am I making sure I'm not the only one doing all the organizational work? Is my family invested into the idea of being a part of getting organized?
- [ ] Are we doing all we can to prepare ahead of time what we need for the next day?
- [ ] Are there other areas where planning could reduce stress in my life—meals, laundry, physical fitness, etc.?

Using the Checklist: Boredom and the Blue Bag
- [ ] Do I have a blue bag?
- [ ] Did I add anything new to the blue bag this month?

Using the Checklist: Over-Programming vs. The Quiet Mind
- [ ] Are we over programmed this month?
- [ ] Have I found a way for my kids to quiet their brains without being bored?
- [ ] Have I assessed every person's individual need to have a down day?
- [ ] Have I scheduled a quiet day?
- [ ] Did I put SSR on the calendar?

Using the Checklist: Chunk it Down
- [ ] What tasks in my home might benefit from being broken down into smaller pieces?
- [ ] Do my children know how to chunk down their homework? Their chores?
- [ ] Do I have Post-its scattered freely about so my family can organize their work?
- [ ] Do I have a list of fun things to do in between the work?

Using the Checklist: Passion
- [ ] Am I pushing my children to do something they don't want to do?
- [ ] Is it my dream or my child's dream?
- [ ] Can I help my children find their passions?
- [ ] Did we try something new this month?
- [ ] Have I accidentally driven a wedge between me and my child by pushing?
- [ ] Do my children enjoy the activities they are doing?

Using the Checklist: Outlining Your Family Values
- [ ] Have we outlined our family values?
- [ ] Have we created a document that represents our family mission statement?
- [ ] Do we need to update it?
- [ ] Is it easy to view and edit for all members of the family?

Using the Checklist: Goal Setting

☐ Do you have a goal or dream board for yourself?

☐ Do your children have goal or dream boards for themselves?

☐ Can you identify three ways you helped your child delay gratification this month?

☐ Have you seen successes, big or small, to remind you that your family goals are working?

Using the Checklist: Yelling and Hitting

☐ Am I currently a yeller or a spanker?

☐ If so, do I want to find new ways to achieve my goals?

☐ What areas of my life currently need adjustment, and how can I create a plan to get that done?

☐ Have I practiced taking a deep breath before yelling lately?

☐ How can I institute consequences for my children's negative behaviors without hitting them?

☐ Do I know how to get help if I need it?

Using the Checklist: Laughter

☐ Are we laughing as a family?

☐ Am I teaching my kids to laugh at themselves?

☐ Can we laugh through adversity?

☐ Can we find something funny about struggling through a problem?

Using the Checklist: The Internet

☐ What are my children seeing on the Internet? Am I taking time to monitor their use?

☐ Am I asking questions about what they are researching online?

☐ Are we learning how to cross-check research so that we aren't accepting one point of view?

☐ Are we collecting electronics every night to eliminate their use in the middle of the night?

☐ Am I warning my kids that the comments that follow an article online are not part of the scientific research or the article?

Using the Checklist: Patterns Outside the Home

☐ Am I calling ahead when my children attend social events? *Remember, this sets up a pattern for later.*

☐ Have I offered to chaperone a party?

☐ Have I started a network of parents to rely on for parties?

☐ Am I offering to help at all the different parties my children attend?

☐ Have I started a Safe Homes agreement at my school?

Using the Checklist: Taking Care of You

- [ ] Am I scheduling so I also have some down time?
- [ ] What have I done for me this month?
- [ ] Am I getting enough sleep and exercise?
- [ ] Do I have a list of dreams and wishes for myself?
- [ ] What am I going to do this month for myself?
- [ ] Does my family have the information they need to help me realize my dreams?

Using the Checklist: Role Modeling

- [ ] Am I being careful to be a good role model, especially when or if I use alcohol?
- [ ] What is the message I'm sending to my child today?

Using the Checklist: Intention

- [ ] Can I spend 5 minutes thinking about the excitement of my children today?

Links:

Our website: www.milestogodrugeducation.com
Additional information for this handbook:
www.milestogodrugeducation.com/motherschecklist

Our first handbook, *Not All Kids Do Drugs*, is available on our
website.

Links: Section 1A

University of Toronto Center for Addiction and Mental Health. (2011, July 1)
An Early Start: Drug Education Begins At Home.. (follow links: About Mental
Health & Addictions: Information about drugs and addiction: Parenting: An Early
Start (web pages) http://camh.net/

Community of Concern. (2011, September 1) *Parenting Tools.*
http://www.thecommunityofconcern.org/ Click on "Parenting Tools"

Links: Section 1B

Marc A. Schuckit, Tom L. Smith, Jon Heron, Matthew Hickman, John Macleod,
Glyn Lewis, John M. Davis, Joseph R. Hibbeln, Sandra Brown, Luisa Zuccolo,
Laura L. Miller, George Davey-Smith. **Testing a Level of Response to Alcohol-
Based Model of Heavy Drinking and Alcohol Problems in 1,905 17-year-olds.**
Alcoholism: Clinical and Experimental Research, 2011; DOI: 10.1111/j.1530-
0277.2011.01536.x

Alcoholism: Clinical & Experimental Research (2011, July 15).
Response to alcohol, peers, expectancies, and coping all contribute to adolescent
drinking. *ScienceDaily*. Retrieved September 24, 2011, from
http://www.sciencedaily.com
/releases/2011/07/110715163211.htm?utm_source=feedburner&utm_medium=em
ail&utm_campaign=Feed%3A+sciencedaily+%28ScienceDaily%3A+Latest+Scie
nce+News%29

Links: Section 2A

Tannen, Deborah. (1990). *You Just Don't Understand, Women and Men in
Conversation*. New York: Ballantine Books. More about Dr. Tannen's work at:
http://www9.georgetown.edu/faculty/tannend/bio.html

Covey, Stephen R. (1989) *The 7 Habits of Highly Effective People*. New York:
Fireside Books. More about Stephen Covey:
https://www.stephencovey.com/7habits/7habits-habit1.php

Merriam-Webster 2011. http://www.merriam-webster.com/

Links: Section 2B
Helmstetter, Shad. (2011) **http://www.shadhelmstetter.com/**

"Vygotsky, Lev Semyonovich." Complete Dictionary of Scientific Biography. 2008. Retrieved September 24, 2011 from Encyclopedia.com: http://www.encyclopedia.com/doc/1G2-2830906184.html

Moorman, Chick. (1998) *Parent Talk: How to Talk to Your Children in Language That Builds Self-Esteem and Encourages Responsibility.* New York: Fireside Books. More about Chick Moorman: http://chickmoorman.com/

Pipher, Mary. (1994) *Reviving Ophelia.* New York: Ballantine Books.

Links: Section 2C

Karp, Harvey. (2004) *The Happiest Toddler on the Block.* New York: Bantam Books. More on Dr. Karp: http://www.happiestbaby.com/

Rimm, Sylvia. (1994) Raising Preschoolers: Parenting for Today. New York: Three Rivers Press. More on Dr. Rimm: **http://www.sylviarimm.com/**

Links: Section 2D

NIDA National Institute on Drug Abuse. Retrieved September 24, 2011. OTC information: http://www.nida.nih.gov/infofacts/PainMed.html

FDA U.S. Food and Drug Administration. (2011, April 7.) *FDA Drug Safety Communication: Reports of a rare, but serious and potentially fatal adverse effect with the use of over-the-counter (OTC) benzocaine gels and liquids applied to the gums or mouth.* Retrieved September 24, 2011. From http://www.fda.gov/Drugs/DrugSafety/ucm250024.htm

Links: Section 2E

BioMed Central (2009, April 24). Herbal Remedy: Teens Often Use Cannabis For Relief, Not Recreation, Study Finds. *ScienceDaily.* Retrieved September 25, 2011, from http://www.sciencedaily.com /releases/2009/04/090422191724.htm#.Tllt9P082gY.email

http://www.medicinenet.com/caffeine/article.htm (retrieved September 2011) All About Caffeine.

Links: Section 3A
Wikipedia.org (Retrieved September 24, 2011). Diana Baumrind: http://en.wikipedia.org/wiki/Diana_Baumrind

Positive-Parenting-Alley.com. (Retrieved September 24, 2011) Diana Baumrind's 3 Parenting Styles: Get a full understanding of the 3 archetypical parents. From http://www.positive-parenting-ally.com/parenting-styles.html

Bahr, Stephen J., Hoffman, John P. 2010. Parenting Style, Religiosity, Peers, and Adolescent Heavy Drinking. Journal of Studies on Alcohol and Drugs, 71, 539-543, 2010)

Cohen DA, Rice J. 1997. US National Library of Medicine National Istitutes of Health. PubMed.gov J Drug Educ. 1997;27(2):199-211. Louisiana State University Medical Center, New Orleans, USA.

Brigham Young University. 2011, June 21. *Teens and Alcohol Study: Parenting style can prevent binge drinking*. Retrieved September 25, 2011 from http://news.byu.edu/archive10-jun-parentingstyle.aspx

Links: Section 3B

Covey, Stephen R. (1989) *The 7 Habits of Highly Effective People*. New York: Fireside Books.More about Stephen Covey: https://www.stephencovey.com/7habits/7habits-habit1.php

Gale, Scott. (2009) *Your Family Constitution*. Irvine, CA. Spectrum International Press.

Severe, Sal. (2002) *How To Behave So Your Preschooler Will Too!* New York. Penguin Books.

McGraw, Jay. (2000*) Life Strategies For Teens*. Clearwater, Florida. Touchtone Books.

Weill Cornell Medical College (2011, September 1). Marshmallow test points to biological basis for delayed gratification#.Tl-WnSJuzfk.email. *ScienceDaily*. Retrieved September 25, 2011, from http://www.sciencedaily.com

Association for Psychological Science (2008, September 11). Why Delaying Gratification Is Smart#.TmuUdhjZpiM.email. *ScienceDaily*. Retrieved September 25, 2011, from http://www.sciencedaily.com /releases/2008/09/080909111022.htm#.TmuUdhjZpiM.email

Links: Section 3C

Society for Research in Child Development (2005, November 14). Spanking Leads To Child Aggression And Anxiety, Regardless Of Cultural Norm. *ScienceDaily*. Retrieved September 25, 2011, from http://www.sciencedaily.com /releases/2005/11/051114110820.htm

Duman, Sarah, Margolin, Gayla. 2009, March 2.Parents' Aggressive Influences and Children's Aggressive Problem Solutions with Peers. J Clin Child Adolesc Psychol. Author manuscript; available in PMC 2009 March 2. Published in final edited form as: J Clin Child Adolesc Psychol. 2007 March; 36(1): 42–55.

Made in the USA
San Bernardino, CA
07 October 2016